Penguin Education X13
Penguin Science of Behaviour
General Editor: B. M. Foss

Method and History
Editor: W. M. O'Neil

The Beginnings of Modern Psychology
W. M. O'Neil

The Beginnings of
Modern Psychology

W. M. O'Neil

Penguin Books
Baltimore · Maryland

Penguin Books Ltd, Harmondsworth,
Middlesex, England
Penguin Books Inc., 7110 Ambassador Road,
Baltimore, Md 21207, U.S.A.
Penguin Books Australia Ltd, Ringwood,
Victoria, Australia

First published 1968
Copyright © W. M. O'Neil, 1968

Made and printed in Great Britain by
Hazell Watson & Viney Ltd,
Aylesbury, Bucks
Set in Linotype Plantin

Penguin Science of Behaviour

This book is one of the first in an ambitious project, the *Penguin Science of Behaviour*, which will cover a very wide range of psychological inquiry. Many of the short 'unit' texts will be on central teaching topics, while others will deal with present theoretical and empirical work which the Editors consider to be important new contributions to psychology. We have kept in mind both the teaching divisions of psychology and also the needs of psychologists at work. For readers working with children, for example, some of the units in the field of Developmental Psychology will deal with techniques in testing children, other units will deal with work on cognitive growth. For academic psychologists, there will be units in well-established areas such as Learning and Perception, but also units which do not fall neatly under any one heading, or which are thought of as 'applied', but which nevertheless are hightly relevant to psychology as a whole.

The project is published in short units for two main reasons. Firstly, a large range of short texts at inexpensive prices gives the teacher a flexibility in planning his course and recommending texts for it. Secondly, the pace at which important new work is published requires the project to be adaptable. Our plan allows a unit to be revised or a fresh unit to be added with maximum speed and minimal cost to the reader.

Above all, for students, the different viewpoints of many authors, sometimes overlapping, sometimes in contradiction, and the range of topics Editors have selected will reveal the complexity and diversity which exist beyond the necessarily conventional headings of an introductory course.

B.M.F.

Contents

Editorial Foreword

The Beginnings of Modern Psychology is the first monograph to be published in the series devoted to history and method in psychology. It is planned to follow it with other monographs written by experts on the several contemporary movements in psychology. Principal amongst these are S–R or behaviourist theory, cognitive theory deriving primarily from Gestalt psychology, dynamic depth psychology embracing both psychoanalytic theory and other views deeply indebted to Freud, information theory applied to organismic behaviour and the multi-variate approach to individual differences in ability and temperament, or, more generally, personality. The present monograph has been written as a backdrop to these studies of contemporary movements.

I propose to write a second monograph as a framework for more detailed studies of various aspects of method in the study of psychology. It will examine the broad features of theorizing and the relations of theory to factual observations on psychology. It will be followed by other monographs written by experts on measurement, experimentation and other observational methods, and on the discussion of those perennial problems such as purposive versus mechanistic explanation, the self or person, and the nature of motivational and cognitive processes.

There will also be a number of monographs straddling the two strands in this series. They will be studies of the methodological and theoretical issues raised by various important contributors to modern psychology. Among the first of these will be an evaluation of the concept of purpose as developed by McDougall, and another will examine the relation of the Gestalt theorists to their antecedents.

Though there is a general plan underlying the writing of this series of monographs, it is intended that each book will stand on its own feet so that the student (and his teacher) will be able to choose those appropriate to his needs without having to turn, in that infuriating way that some dictionaries demand, to other items in the series.

W.M. O'N.

1 Introduction

The word 'psychology', though modern, is older than the subject it now names. It is composed of Greek elements, but it is not Greek. It was created in the fifteenth century to refer to one aspect of the study of spiritual being. The whole study was called pneumatology and psychology was the part concerned with the human soul. In 1732 Christian von Wolff used the word to denote the secular philosophical analysis and interpretation of mental phenomena. David Hartley in 1748 used the word in English with the same meaning. Some time in the latter half of the nineteenth century its reference shifted from a predominantly philosophic to a predominantly scientific study of mental phenomena. It is in this more recent sense that it is being used here. Some philosophers, especially in continental Europe, wish to preserve von Wolff's and Hartley's usage. However, almost everywhere else those who speak of themselves as psychologists think of their subject not as a speculative discipline within philosophy but as a member of the family of empirical sciences. It is for them a body of knowledge derived from systematic observation and organized by thought. It is concerned with a subject matter lying in the borderlands of the biological sciences and the social sciences. This subject matter used to be spoken of as the mind but it is now usually referred to as behaviour. This represents a conceptual and not merely a verbal change.

Scientific psychology emerged about a hundred years ago, though it is difficult to specify a birth date. It is common to speak of Wilhelm Wundt (1832–1920) as the founder of scientific psychology. He certainly has the credit for the first laboratory, which was officially established in 1879, for teaching and research in the subject.

His *Philosophische Studien*, begun in 1881, was the first periodical devoted to the publication of experimental studies. Bain's journal *Mind* was earlier (1876), but though devoted to psychology it was hardly a journal for observational studies as was Wundt's. Finally, Wundt's *Grundzüge der physiologischen Psychologie* (1st edition, 1874), has strong claims to being the first general handbook in the modern vein; earlier systematic treatments had tended to be either clearly physiological if experimental in temper or clearly philosophical if concerned mainly with problems of the mind.

There are many precursors to Wundt for whom a claim to founding an experimental psychology might be made. Gustav Fechner (1801–87) certainly established psychophysics and in so doing made a very great methodological contribution to the emerging experimental psychology. However, he was concerned with the specific problem of the relation of mind to matter rather than with psychology in general. Hermann von Helmholtz (1821–94) had a more general interest which in the light of his contributions gives him a greater claim. It must be admitted that he was primarily a physicist and a physiologist and that his psychological work was an extension of his pursuit of those other interests. As selfconscious a science as psychology can be satisfied only with a whole-hearted founder. Were we to take Fechner as its only true begetter, we could name 1860 as psychology's birth date, for in that year his *Elemente der Psychophysik* appeared. The choice of Helmholtz might yield 1866, the date of the completed publication of his *Handbuch der physiologischen Optik*. Though not an experimentalist, Alexander Bain (1818–1903) had so many ideas acceptable to later experimenters that his two books, *The Senses and the Intellect* and *The Emotions and the Will*, appearing respectively in 1855 and 1859, might seem to some to mark some sort of birthday in instalments. He is more appropriately regarded as one of the last of the old style than the first of the modern style psychologists. A claim might be made for Francis

Galton (1822–1911) who initiated many observational studies of psychological problems and devised methods for their conduct. However he formulated few, if any, general psychological views. His claim to be recognized as a founding father of statistics or even differential psychology is on much more solid ground than any claim that may be made for his role in founding modern observational psychology. Were he to be chosen, 1869 (*Hereditary Genius*) would be a suitable date.

The truth of the matter is that the difficulty in specifying a birthday does not reside so much in the problem of saying who was Zeus as in the fact that modern psychology did not spring fully armed from the head of anyone. Ebbinghaus said in 1908 that psychology had a long past but only a short history. Though another sixty years has been added to the history of psychology his remark is still true, and the turning point between past and history is still indeterminate.

Psychology as a methodical observational study began with the application of methods, mainly experimental, derived largely from physiology to problems derived largely from philosophy. As it developed it built up by invention, by borrowing and by adaptation fairly distinctive technical methods. Many of the problems with which it began turned out not to be amenable to the experimental method. Some were abandoned and some were reformulated so as to render them accessible to the experimental method. But far outnumbering the bequeathed problems are quite new ones encountered in the course of trying to deal with the old.

The past also bequeathed to modern psychology a number of ways of conceiving mental phenomena and a number of specific preconceptions. The rejection, the replacement, the modification and the re-adopting of these notions largely makes up the history of modern psychological thought, at any rate the part of psychology's history that is most worth telling. An account of the introduction of particular techniques and of the discovery of particular facts is by itself of limited value. The body of factual knowledge and the repertoire of methods are better set out in systematically organized handbooks than in a chronological order.

From the long past of psychology came a major and a minor philosophical influence. The former derived from the British empiricist movement as it was expressed in associationism. The source of mind was held by those in this movement to be experience of the world around; mind was indeed no more than the collection and combination of the sensations gained in such experience and of the images in which sensations were re-evoked. The minor influence derived from faculty theory and a number of companion trends, all of which were strongly tinged with rationalism. Some of these rationalist doctrines go back to scholastic elaborations of Aristotle or even to Plato, but it is from more modern exponents that the influence mainly comes. Whereas Wundt worked within the context of the associationist empiricist tradition, Franz Brentano (1838–1917), who offered an alternative conception of psychology, represented the tradition with a rationalist flavour. It is from the latter tradition that the two-part division of mental functions into noetic and orectic (sometimes further divided into cognition, conation and affection) and the notion of higher and lower levels of mental activity came. Much of the stock in trade of the modern typologists and differential psychologists has the same predominantly rationalist origin.

From the more recent past came a considerable influence from the rapidly growing physiology of the senses and of the nervous system. The influence on psychology has always been strongest from the experimental side of the basic medical sciences, though a not unimportant influence has been exercised especially in this century from the clinical side of medicine. But we shall need to consider first the line of work running from Charles Bell (1774–1842) through Johannes Müller (1801–58) to Helmholtz, before we examine the influences derived from a long line of French physicians and expressed principally through Sigmund Freud (1856–1939).

The philosophical tradition of associationism was already present in the sensory physiology of Müller and Helmholtz. What Wundt did was to work out more thoroughly the implications of this conjunction. His was a physiological psychology mainly because he applied the methods of experimental sensory physiology to the problems addressed by associationism and still formulated by him in essentially associationist terms.

While Wundt and a numerous band of like-minded persons were setting up an experimental psychology of mental content, two other influences came to work, not so much upon those within that movement as upon those who approved of the experimental approach to mental events but not of the Wundtian conception of them. Wundtian psychology, as did British associationism, set out to provide an account of mental experience in terms of elementary experiences. Thus it was concerned with mental content or phenomena in the technical sense of that term, that is, appearances. The task was akin to that of chemistry in identifying elementary content and in showing how these elements were added and combined in the experiences of everyday life. Others believed that a more dynamic, a more active conception of mind was required. On the continent of Europe such a conception was put forward as act psychology, first by Franz Brentano, who was predominantly a philosopher, and later by Carl Stumpf (1848–1936) and others more inclined to experimentation. In America William James (1842–1910) was an early spokesman and following him were the functionalists like James Angell (1869–1949) and Harvey Carr (1873–1954) at Chicago, and Edward Thorndike (1874–1949) and Robert S. Woodworth (1869–1962) at Columbia. That act psychology and functionalism had much in common is evidenced by their intermingling in Britain in G. F. Stout (1860–1944) and W. McDougall (1871–1938), the former more act psychologist, the latter more functionalist but both clearly of the same genus. Act psychology stressed mental processes as activities: the mental was the sensing rather than the sensed, the perceiving rather than the perceived, the judging rather than the judged, the feeling rather than the felt. Functionalism was also concerned with mind in action, with a person coping with his surroundings, responding to them and working on them so that he might survive in them. Act psychology had a stronger philosophical flavour than functionalism though the latter had some philosophical inclinations. Act psychology usually adopted the phenomenological viewpoint which was elaborated by the philosopher Husserl but stemmed from Brentano with whom Husserl had studied. Functionalism had a strong affinity, missing in act psychology, for the practical and was almost always placed in a broad biological setting, a characteristic found only occasionally, and then in Britain rather than on the Continent, in act psychology. The underlying differences between act psychology and functionalism are easier to see in their offspring *Gestalttheorie* and the wider *Ganzheit* movement in Europe on the one hand and American behaviourism on the other.

The contemporaneous influences important for the opposition to Wundtianism were the evolutionary theory of Charles Darwin (1809–82) on the one hand, and on the other the philosophical realist movement of the late nineteenth and early twentieth centuries which tried to work out an empiricism without becoming enmeshed in phenomenalism as Locke, Berkeley and Hume had been.

Darwinism stressed the adaptability of the living organism, the relevance of this adaptability for survival and the essential unity of the whole animal kingdom. These conceptions became the central inspiration of functionalism. Darwin emphasized individual variation within species and the transmission of these variations through inheritance. Francis Galton was prompted by these considerations to embark on a wide-ranging series of studies which we now recognize as the beginnings of differential psychology.

The philosophical influence in the latter half of the nineteenth century is more difficult to unravel. James, who was the precursor of American functionalism, was a leading exponent of the new empiricism and clearly an influence on American new realism which had so much to do with the early radical behaviourism of the 1920s. This realist movement was strong too in Britain. Though not a wholehearted member of it, Stout obviously belonged to it. Stout too was influenced by Darwinism. Continental act psychology was left untouched at first by evolutionary theory, though its derivatives show the influence clearly enough in the various attempts to show the parallel of phylogeny and ontogeny. Act psychology being more philosophical than functionalism was influenced by, or perhaps was a manifestation of, the new empiricism. However it had deeper roots in the scholastic views with which faculty theory was associated: the mind is to be defined in terms of its structure and powers, potential and actual, rather than in terms of its content or the objects of its 'minding'.

Contemporary psychology has felt one other great influence lying outside the traditions working within it in the nineteenth century. This comes from psychological medicine, a field attracting near quacks like Friedrich Mesmer (1734–1815) as well as genuine scientists. Now and then medical psychology found a meeting ground with philosophical psychology as in David Hartley (1705–57) or with experimental psychology as in Alfred Binet (1857–1911), but by and large it developed along separate lines. The powerful contributions in clinical observation and theoretical interpretations by Jean Charcot (1825–93), Pierre Janet (1859–1947), Morton Prince (1854–1929) and above all Sigmund Freud could not forever remain outside the experimental tradition. Though medical psychology continues to be somewhat separate, it has come to be a member of the complex society of modern psychology.

The history to be recounted in the following pages is of a city founded in the seventh and eighth decades of the eighteenth century on a very old site. Many of the remains of older settlements have been built into the present structures. In its short history there has been much rebuilding and the city boundaries have changed; what were once smarter areas have become dilapidated and neglected, and the foci of life within the city have changed. Political activity has always been vigorous, new parties have been formed, old ones have waned, and the constitution has been revised many times. In addition to all this action and counteraction within, there has been one major invasion and several minor invasions from without. Though largely assimilated now, the invaders have preserved much of their own outlook and ways of life. They have found common cause with some of the old inhabitants, the citizens now being divided into four major ideological groups each with some subdivisions. At one extreme are those who see man largely as an animal or even as a machine, if there be any difference between animal and machine. At the other are those who see him as a person, as a fellow being with beliefs, expectancies and intentions. The former are the biotropes to whom mechanism has an increasing appeal and to whom the discovery of laws, akin to those in the physical and natural sciences, is a prime concern. The latter are sociotropes for whom teleological conceptions are generally more congenial and who tend to be suspicious of contentions about the lawfulness of behaviour even if they are not outright supporters of an idiographic view of human personality.

The main group of biotropes consist of those who see the future of psychology assured only if it can be firmly attached to a neurophysiological and biochemical base. Akin to them, though often more mechanotropic than biotropic, are the S–R theorists or behaviourists and a more recently arisen group interpreting behaviour in terms of information theory. The most extreme of the personalists are the dynamic depth psychologists – psychoanalytic theorists and others springing from or deeply influenced by Freud. In between lies a third group, sometimes finding common cause with liberal behaviourists, sometimes with dynamic depth psychologists, but often standing aloof. They are the cognitive theorists, the spokesmen for a psychology of content but one quite unlike the elementarist version originally propounded by Wundt. There is a fourth group, often in coalition with one of the others. Its members are less concerned with giving an account of man in action than with classifying and measuring intellectual and temperamental characteristics which differ from individual to individual.

The task of this monograph is to see how these divisions among the citizens arose.

2 The Long Philosophical Past

A good deal of the history of early modern philosophy can be told in terms of the opposing movements, rationalism and empiricism. It is not easy, however, to say in a few pages without grave danger of misrepresentation just what are the central views of these two opposing movements. Each embraces a variety of tenets and any particular philosopher's opinions are likely to be a mixture rather than a pure expression of either set. What concerns us most here are certain views about the nature, the sources and the validity of human knowledge and about the nature and the conditions of existence. That is, answers to epistemological and ontological questions are central for the present purpose.

It may be best to begin with one of these questions. How, for instance, can we justify or support some belief or some alleged knowledge? One resort, often made in medieval times, was to authority. Another, also favoured in that period, was to axiomatic or self-evident truths. René Descartes (1596–1650), often regarded as the first great modern philosopher, recognized that turning to authorities still left one with the problem of justifying the belief in those authorities. Further, he called into question, in a critical way which has become characteristic of the modern period, many of the allegedly axiomatic truths. He considered the only bedrock upon which to build were axioms able to survive this critical scrutiny. For example, a man cannot reasonably doubt that he is conscious. If he is conscious, it follows that he must exist – *cogito ergo sum*. This Descartes took to be a necessary truth or a situation which could not in itself be otherwise. Such a belief in and the consequent search for necessary truths about the world is distinctively rationalistic.

John Locke (1632–1704), an early spokesman of empiricism, maintained that the justification of our beliefs must be found in our sensory experience. His successors, notably David Hume (1711–76), argued against the notion of necessary truths, maintaining that any real event could conceivably have been different from what it in fact was. Thus, factual truth was deemed by Hume always to be contingent. The rationalist admitted the apparent contingency of most situations that we know, but looked for some necessary truths upon which the apparently contingent ultimately depended. The extreme empiricists regarded all truths as being contingent in the sense that they involved mere conjunctions not dependent upon anything which was not itself contingent.

In contrasting the views of Descartes and Locke one needs to distinguish two distinct questions. The first concerns the source of our knowledge and the second the backing for it. Descartes believed that much of our knowledge, in particular our knowledge of the axiomatic, is inborn. He believed that we know it from the beginning and do not have to learn it from our observations of events about us. Locke denied this, asserting that the mind begins as a blank sheet and that what we know has been written there by experience. We have already seen their answers to the second question. Descartes's answer to the first question is spoken of as 'nativism' whereas his answer to the second is 'rationalism', and Locke's answers to both questions have been commonly called 'empiricism'. In German, there are two words *empiristisch* and *empirisch* providing different verbal symbols for Locke's answers to the two questions. Those writers in English who have tried to duplicate this linguistic distinction seem justified in doing so. Hence, in the following discussion 'empiristic' will mean the opposite of 'nativistic' and 'empiricist' the opposite of 'rationalist'. Nativism does not commit one to rationalism though it has an affinity with it because it is helpful to it.

Parallel with the distinction between the necessary and

the contingent is a distinction between a fundamental kind of existence, which is the essence or immutable core of a thing, and the dependent, changing manifestations of this underlying reality. Reason is deemed to be our mental instrument of access to the fundamental; sense-perception is deemed to give access only to the superficial dependent reality. Rationalism favours this distinction and empiricism often opposes it.

Once one denies that sensible qualities have other than a dependent existence, one is readily involved in denying them any basic existence. In this way the rationalist is inclined to believe in some single reality, some Absolute beyond which there is nothing else. Paradoxically at first sight, those who begin by asserting two levels of existence often end by asserting a single existence, whereas those who assert a single way of existing must, if they are to say anything about anything, assert many independent existences. To say that roses are red may be deemed to involve us in asserting the separate existence of rose and of red, unless we maintain that somehow red emerges from the inner nature of roses. The doctrine of multiple separate existences is called pluralism.

The Rationalist Heritage

Modern psychology, being predominantly empiricist in spirit, has been directly influenced by rationalism only when some part of that doctrine has been in a predominantly empiricist context. This renders difficult the giving of a simple account of what exercised the influence and of how it was exercised.

Many of these influences can be traced to the medieval formulation of Aristotelian views. Neo-scholasticism has been the immediate donor in several instances, though more frequently the influence has been exercised by thinkers who might be startled by the recognition of themselves as the carriers of a scholastic inheritance.

Related to Aristotle's distinction between substance and

form, which are not, as it were, two separate entities but rather features of one and the same thing, was his distinction between the potential and the actual. There is the abiding power of seeing, but only from time to time is there some specific act of seeing – a making actual of the potential. The scholastics were concerned to enumerate these powers, or faculties as they came to be called. Not every act of seeing was the manifestation of a separate potentiality; indeed the point of the doctrine was to bring out the unity in multiplicity rather than to fragment the mind. Aristotle's distinction between the vegetative, the animal and the rational living principles (souls) provided the inspiration for the stratification of the faculties. Thus Sense-perception was a lower and Reason a higher power. Perhaps the hierarchical organization of the Church made the scholastics prone to find hierarchies elsewhere. Aristotle also provided a distinction between noetic and orectic functions, between knowledge and desire. Thus a fourfold division of faculties was common in later medieval thought, such as:

	Noetic	Orectic
Higher	Reason	Will
Lower	Sensation	Impulse

Sometimes orexis was divided into active (conative) and passive (affective) to yield the tripartite division of mental phenomena which found much favour in continental Europe in the seventeenth, eighteenth and nineteenth centuries and in Britain in the late nineteenth and early twentieth. Cognition, affection and conation were accepted by Stout as the basic modes of consciousness and by McDougall as the basic aspects of mental process.

Faculty theory was finally banished in name from modern psychology, but the problems with which it was concerned, reformulated in various ways, were adopted by differential psychology. Francis Galton who began this branch of modern psychology even preserved the word 'faculty'. What is more important, he preserved in a more empiricist setting many of the conceptions of faculty theory. Spearman (1863–1945), the first systematist of differential psychology, though overtly rejecting faculty theory itself, consciously adopted many of its components, for example, the distinction between noetic and orectic (as well as the use of these words), the relativist definition of factors (faculties) in terms of what they do rather than of what they are, the rejection of an elementarism of content, the inclination to regard factors as immutable (innate in this case), and finally a preference for hierarchical classification.

However, scholasticism exerted a stronger influence through those who eliminated or at least diluted the faculty element. Their stress was on the mental act as distinct from the mental content, on the unity and uniqueness of the ego and on its self-determination. The early modern rationalists like Descartes and Leibniz (1646–1716), even when rejecting the major philosophical views of the scholastics, continued and sometimes accentuated a number of their tendencies. Though Descartes sharply distinguished body and mind in a way quite at odds with scholastic doctrine, he helped to preserve the mind from the onslaughts of mechanism, which was already showing some promise of being able to deal with bodily processes. Leibniz had his strongest effect upon psychology through Christian von Wolff (1679–1754), who attempted a systematization of psychology firstly in rationalist terms and secondly as a body of factual knowledge. In doing so, von Wolff gave a modern statement of faculty theory. He distinguished between the powers of the mind and the faculties; the latter were regarded as mere potencies of action whereas the former consisted 'in the continual endeavour to act', an activist notion which tends to assert itself in almost every opposition to associationist and related mechanist movements in modern psychology. A distinctive power of the mind was held by von

Wolff to be the *vis repraesentiva*: the power and urge of the mind to represent to itself the objects which affect the sense organs. He adopted the threefold division of the faculties – cognitive, affective and conative. Though Immanual Kant (1724–1804) rejected the faculty notion, he accepted von Wolff's division of mental acts and passed it on to many of the philosophically minded psychologists of the late nineteenth century.

As we shall see, associationism viewed mind as mechanistic, as passive and as divisible into a multiplicity of elementary contents. In contrast, rationalism conceived mind as an active, purposive and unitary agent which engaged in knowing, feeling and striving. Further, it maintained a distinction between the animal powers we share with lower creatures and the higher powers which are distinctive of human minds, and it was reluctant to accept any simplifying or reducing of mental experiences from the form in which we have them. Whenever a modern psychologist, no matter how empiricist in spirit, has wished to castigate associationism, he has ordinarily turned to the rationalists' cupboard for a suitable stick. This applies to Reid and others in the Scottish school who opposed Humean associationism, to Brentano and the other act psychologists who opposed Wundt, to Ward and Stout who opposed the last flourish of British associationism as expressed by Bain, to James and the later American functionalists who opposed a variety of associationist doctrines and started an associationism of their own, and finally to the Gestalt movement which began in Germany in opposition to the remnants of Wundtianism and ended in America equally vigorous in attack on behaviourism, the associationism indigenous to that country.

British Empiricism and Associationism

The associationist movement, running from Locke and Berkeley to Mill and Bain, was so closely connected with the empiricist philosophy of Locke, Berkeley and Hume that the two lines of thought tend to be treated as one. However, it seems better to make a distinction between the two, since the elaboration of the associationist doctrine occurred largely after the working out of the main lines of the empiricist position.

Locke set out to clarify an epistemological problem and in the course of doing so he sketched the ground plan of a psychology. As part of the argument for the view that we need to justify our beliefs on a basis of sensory experience, he maintained that our sense experience is a principal (if not the sole) source of knowledge. What we have in knowledge are, he held, the impressions external objects make upon us. We do not know directly the objects which make these impressions; we know only the states of mind (ideas) they set up in us. These states may correspond with the external objects and so, in knowing the former, we have some indirect knowledge of the latter. Those who later pushed this view to the extreme were forced to dispense altogether with statements about external objects and were left only with claims about ideas – such a view is termed subjective idealism. Locke maintained that knowledge consists of simple ideas which are not analysable into other ideas and complex ideas which are composed of simple ideas linked in temporal trains or in synchronous complexes. In this proposition Locke asserted the central tenet of associationism.

Locke accepted three distinct terms in his analysis: a mind which has knowledge, its ideas (i.e., whatever it thinks of) and external objects. Though having ideas was frequently treated by him as a passive occurrence (a view adopted in a more thorough-going way by his successors), he often spoke of mind as active, speaking of mental powers in a way not unlike that adopted by faculty theory. Ideas, such as 'whiteness, hardness, ... man, elephant ...', he maintained derived either from sensation (ideas of the external world) or from the mind's reflection on its own operations. The latter is akin to the inner sense more characteristic of faculty and self psychologies than of associationism. From the examination of certain illusory experiences, Locke came to the opinion that sensations were experiences produced in the mind by the action of objects and were not literally an experiencing of the object. Following Galileo, he held that the sensory quality corresponds to some property in the object itself only in some cases. Where this occurs, for example objects extended in three dimensions produce a sensation of solidity, the impression (idea) is of a primary quality. In other cases the sensory quality corresponds in no way to the properties of the object which produce that quality. For example high pitched sound is produced by rapid vibration and low pitched sound by slow vibration, yet our impression is of pitch and not of rate of vibration. Sounds, like colours, tastes and smells, are secondary qualities.

Berkeley (1685–1753) recognized that this argument about secondary qualities could be applied to primary qualities. If it can be argued that the impression of colour resides only in the mind, the same can be argued for the impression of solidity or extension. Though some ideas may correspond to reality, we have no way of knowing that to be so, if all we know are ideas. In this way Berkeley retained the mind and its ideas but dispensed with the external objects and in so doing purified the idealism implicit in Locke. 'To be, is to be known,' said Berkeley – *esse est percipi*: there is no being outside being known. Locke accounted for the regularity and orderliness of our ideas by attributing them to the regularity and orderliness of external events. Berkeley could do so only by maintaining that as God also had these ideas he imposed the order. Hume (1711–76) took the further step in this line of argument. If all we know are ideas, there can be no place for what Berkeley called notions such as mind and God; all there can be are ideas passing in trains. A connected series of trains of ideas constitutes a mind. A mind does not have ideas: it is ideas. Hume incidentally did not continue to use the word 'idea' in this broad sense. He distinguished between impressions (sensations in a later terminology) and ideas (images). Not subscribing to a view of there being both impressions (mental states) and objects (independently existing external events), he could not make the distinction between impressions and ideas in terms of an object present to the senses and of an object absent, as Locke could. Instead he did so in terms of vivacity or vividness – a distinction which observation does not support other than in an approximate way.

Dispensing with God as well as with external objects, Hume could not take Berkeley's resort in accounting for the orderliness of experience. This led him to the reformulation of the laws of association which were implicit in Locke's discussion and went back to Aristotle. The attraction between ideas, Hume held, is due to their resemblance one to another, or to their original contiguity in space and time, or to their being in the relation of cause and effect. Hume's analysis of causation left the third of these laws with an anomalous status; subsequent associationists tended not to subscribe to it, though they tried almost every possible reduction and expansion of the laws of association. A law of contiguity found a place in every list, other frequent entries being laws of similarity, of contrast and of frequency.

Berkeley is best known for his statement of subjective idealism. This doctrine made a deep impress on modern psychology, though the less consistent and milder form of idealism (or phenomenalism) – which treats our sensory perceptions as representations of external objects – has usually been more attractive to psychology. Even more directly important for psychology was Berkeley's analysis of the visual perception of size and distance, an analysis described by Brett as 'the most significant contribution to psychology produced in the eighteenth century' ('Peters's edn, 1953, p. 409). It established a mode of analysis and of explanation which was followed by associationism in its philosophical phase and in its later experimental form in Wundtianism. By Berkeley's time the geometry of vision was well worked out but was being asked to bear too much weight in explaining a variety of phenomena. It is true, for instance, that two objects of different size but at the same distance from the eye will project retinal images different in size. This fact could well be the basis of our perceiving them as being of different size. However, two objects of different size may, if placed at appropriate distances (closer for the smaller object), project the same sized retinal images because they subtend the same visual angle. They ought, then, on the previous argument to appear the same size, but in fact they do not ordinarily do so. If we could judge their distances in some way, we might by inference or even by association arrive at the correct estimation of their size. But how can we see, by means of a two-dimensional retina, the distance of an object from us? Berkeley argued that literally we cannot. We can, however, get what we now call cues to distance, a list Berkeley worked out along present lines. He argued that we do not consciously make an inference from these, but that through their connexion with the experience of distance obtained from touch we have a mediated yet instantaneous experience of distance. This was a clear statement of the empiristic doctrine in associationist terms.

Hume pursued a similar line of argument about our apprehension of causation, trying to reduce our impression that there is an active agent at work to an experience of a regular succession of events. Hume also argued that many other experiences could be reduced to the association of simple ideas, thus setting the pattern for the systematic associationists. The first of these was David Hartley (1705–57), a physician with philosophical and theological interests. One remarkable feature of his associationism was the physiological basis he provided for ideas. The effect of external objects on the sense organs was thought by him to be the initiation of minute vibrations or vibratiuncles in the nerves. Any re-arousals of the given pattern of vibratiuncles would be an evocation of the original experience. The theory is quite fantastic in detail though remarkably prescient in broad outline of the volleys of impulses and of the reverberatory circuits of contemporary neurological theory. Hartley set out in methodical fashion an account of (i) the sensory phenomena of touch, taste, smell, sight and hearing; (ii) the ideational phenomena of meaning, assent, memory, imagination (reverie and dreams) and reason; and (iii) the affective phenomena which he discussed largely as pleasures and pains. Though the data are sketchy, the topics are those of treatises written in the late nineteenth century and early twentieth century. When one remembers the nonsense which Kepler had earlier mixed into his astronomical writings and which Newton put in his metaphysical writings, which he took as seriously as his physics, one is inclined to forgive Hartley for his vibrations and vibratiuncles in the nerves as a means of accounting for sensations and ideas and for the many faulty pieces of observation and analysis with which his *Observations on Man* abound. An instance of the latter occurs in the passage:

The [sense of] taste may be distinguished into two kinds. ... viz. the particular exquisite one, which resides in the tongue, and especially in the tip of it; and the general one, which extends itself to the insides of the lips and cheeks, to the palate, fauces, oesophagus, stomach, and whole alimentary duct, quite down to the anus (1749, p. 151).

Unfortunately Hartley made virtually little immediate impact despite several champions. He found a later protagonist in James Mill (1773–1836). Mill was as thoroughgoing an associationist as Hartley but, though less credulous, he was by training and by experience less equipped to found a truly observational psychology. It was he (perhaps because the time was riper) who had the more marked influence on psychology as we know it. His son, John Stuart Mill, in his Preface to his 1869 edition of

the *Analysis of the Phenomena of the Human Mind*
(originally published in 1829), says: 'At an early period of
Mr Mill's philosophical life, Hartley's work had taken a
strong hold of his mind; and in the maturity of his
powers he formed and executed the purpose of following
up Hartley's leading thought, and completing what
that thinker had begun.' Wisely he dropped Hartley's
attempted physiological account of association. Contemporaneous physiological knowledge was unequal to the
task, though Mill would not have known whether it were
or not. There was a good deal to be said about the physiology of sensation, but Mill shows little evidence of
acquaintance with the new sense physiology as it was
summarized and interpreted, for example, by Johannes
Müller only a few years later. Mill's is a completely mental psychology. However, it is in no way a systematically
observational psychology.

Like Hartley's, Mill's approach to mental phenomena
is classificatory and analytic. Mental phenomena, or feelings as he more commonly called them, are in degree either
simple or complex and in kind either sensory or ideational. The complex feelings are composed of the simple,
and the ideational are derived from the sensory of which
they are copies or images. Sensations occur only in the
presence of objects to the senses, whereas ideas may occur
in their absence. In discussing sensation Mill emphasized
the distinction between the organ (the eye, the ear, etc.),
the sensation (the colour, the sound, etc.) and the object
to which the sensation is referred (the flower, the bell,
etc.). This is not as thorough an analysis as some later
psychologists favoured: there is no distinction between
distal and proximal stimuli or between the receptors
proper and the ancillary mechanisms of the sense organs.
In fact he disclaimed the need to detail the particulars of
the sense organs – a view with which the later experimentalists disagreed. He made no attempt to give an
exhaustive account of the variety of sensations within
any one modality, though he admits the fact of variety.

So although there is a more modern flavour in his providing a section on each of the five traditional senses as well as on muscular and alimentary sensations, there is nothing in the treatment to suggest what was to come. He was clearly not at home in science in its observational, much less experimental, aspects.

After one chapter of the sketchy sensory material, his book launches into its main concern – ideas and the association of ideas. This forms the basis of the treatment of all the complex mental phenomena analysed in the remaining twenty-one chapters.

Thought succeeds thought; idea follows idea, incessantly. If our senses are awake, we are continually receiving sensations, of the eye, the ear, the touch, and so forth; but not sensations alone. After sensations, ideas are perpetually excited of sensations formerly received; after these ideas, other ideas: and during the whole of our lives, a series of these two states of consciousness, called sensations, and ideas, is constantly going on (1878, vol. 1, p. 70).

Feelings, sensory and ideational, occur in two kinds of complex order, the synchronous and the successive. Trains of ideas are an example of the latter and concepts (the taking together in time of several ideas) an example of the former. In all cases these associations occur through the original contiguity of the component feelings.

With Procrustean efficiency Mill fitted all mental phenomena to this frame. Language is the association of words with the ideas of objects; predication is the association of subject and predicate; memory is the evocation, in accordance with associations, of ideas of formerly sensed objects; and so on. On strictly Humean lines mind is equated with the totality of an associated set of feelings. Mind is not some entity which has feelings. Nor, for that matter, are feelings things one has. There are feelings, sensory and ideational, simple and complex, successively and synchronously connected; and that is all there is to the matter. There is no mental agent. Nor is there any dynamic beyond association.

When the idea of Pleasure is associated with an action of our own as its cause; that is, contemplated as the consequent of a certain action of ours, and incapable of otherwise existing; or when the cause of a Pleasure is contemplated as the consequent of an action of ours, and not capable of otherwise existing; a peculiar state of mind is generated which as it is a tendency to action, is properly denominated M O T I V E (ibid., vol 2, p. 258).

This bringing of action or movement within the ambit of association was more fully developed by Bain (1818–1903). Though not an observer in any methodical and controlled way himself, he nevertheless wrote much more like the later experimentalists than did James Mill. Perhaps it would be more accurate to say that he wrote like a field naturalist. In common with John Stuart Mill, Bain felt the inadequacy of James Mill's purely summative view of complex feelings. In chemical terms, James Mill found the notion of mixtures adequate, whereas they argued for the notion of compounds as well. Wundt followed them in this as we shall see. Bain, too, conceived mind in more active terms than did James Mill, being influenced to a greater extent by the vestiges of rationalism in the mental philosophies of Reid and Stewart. Finally Bain did what the new experimental psychologists were doing roughly at the same time, namely trying to base his psychology on a firm neurophysiological foundation. It will be necessary before we turn to the new psychologists to see what neurophysiology was able to provide for them to build upon.

Note

Writers in English up to about 1900 had difficulty in settling on a generic term for mental phenomena. Though 'feeling', 'idea', 'impression' and 'thought' were used by most to designate a species of mental content or mental process, each word was used by one or another theorist for the whole genus of mental phenomena.

3 The Immediate Physiological Background

The Sensory Motor Arc

Though Descartes in his account of the body as a machine introduced the notion of automatic reflexes, it was Robert Whytt (1714–66), a Scottish physiologist, who put it in its modern form. Incidentally, he introduced the terms 'stimulus' and 'response' in which the notion is now customarily stated. Whytt demonstrated that the legs of a decapitated frog but not of a pithed frog made automatic withdrawal movements upon being pinched or pricked. This clearly showed the dependence of such reflexes upon the spinal cord. The more detailed understanding of the neural mechanism awaited the discovery by Charles Bell (1772–1842) of what has come to be known as the Bell–Magendie law. In 1811 Bell showed experimentally, though the later experiments (1822) of Magendie (1783–1855) were more conclusive, that the peripheral spinal nerves are separable into a sensory or afferent set and a motor or efferent set, the former joining the cord dorsally and the latter emerging ventrally. He later showed that this functional differentiation applied to the cranial nerves and he suggested that there might be separate location of sensory and motor functions in the brain. Bell's work led him to support the view that there was a muscle sense in addition to the traditional five. He considered this sense to be important in the control of on-going movement, creating the 'nervous circle', as he called it, or 'feed back', as the jargon of today would put it.

Marshall Hall (1790–1859) extended the knowledge of reflex movement through his experiments on decapitated and spinally sectioned newts and snakes. He distinguished four kinds of movement: voluntary movement which was dependent upon the cerebrum, respiratory movement dependent upon a centre in the medulla, reflex movement which was dependent solely on the spinal cord, and involuntary movement which resulted from direct stimulation of the muscles. He showed that the neural mechanism for some reflexes lay within a single segment of the cord, that for some it straddled two or more segments and that for others a control is exercised from above the segment or segments in which the afferent and efferent nerves concerned are located.

At this time there was no recognition of separate neurones synapsing to form chains and networks; this discovery, made by Cajal in 1889, remained in dispute for some time even after that date. It was, however, recognized that the nerves were not, as had been thought earlier, tubules along which animal spirits flowed. The experiments of Galvani (1791) had shown that electrical changes were involved in the innervation of muscular movement and that movement could be induced by electric discharges from a Leyden jar. It remained to be shown what was the precise nature of the change passing along the nerve fibres and what was the velocity of this passage. Though Dubois-Reymond threw a little light on the former problem in the fifth decade of the century and Bernstein a great deal more by the seventh decade, the membrane theory was not explicitly stated until the beginning of the twentieth century. Progress was more rapid in dealing with the problem of velocity. There was much speculation, some quite wild, about the velocity of the nervous impulse during the first half of the century. Helmholtz in 1850 made the first adequate determination. For the motor-nerve of the frog, his method was to measure the latency of muscular response to electrical stimulation of nerve fibres of given length. The delicacy of the task may be appreciated upon considering that the fibre lengths were around 50 and 60 millimetres and the latencies around 0·002 seconds. Helmholtz's determination lay in the region 25 to 43 metres per second. Recent determinations show different velocities for different fibres ranging from 120 metres per second for the fastest fibres to one metre per second for the slowest. Helmholtz later attempted to measure the velocity of the impulse in the sensory nerve by resorting to the reaction time experiment introduced by the astronomers.

As a means of setting time more accurately than is possible by means of the most refined mechanical clock, astronomers long ago resorted to the observation of the transit of given stars across the meridian. By the late eighteenth century, a procedure had been developed which used a telescope mounted on an east–west axis perpendicular to the vertical passing through the earth's centre. The visual field of the observer was divided by cross-hairs located in the eye-piece. The observer noted the clock reading as the star in its apparent motion (due to the earth's rotation) approached the central line and counted the clock beats up to the actual crossing. In 1795 an assistant at Greenwich was dismissed because of his incorrigible tardiness of up to 0·8 seconds in making this observation as compared with Maskelyne, the Astronomer Royal. The German astronomer Bessel some twenty-five years later became interested in the general question of such differences between observers and produced clear evidence that they were both marked and not due to carelessness in following the prescriptions of the method. Astronomers were still investigating the problem in the eighteen sixties and seventies, by which time the physiologists had become interested. It was Donders (1818–89) who then added such complications to this simple reaction time as discrimination and choice reaction times in the hope of measuring the speed of some of the higher mental processes by the subtraction of simple reaction time from the appropriate complex reaction time. These ideas were elaborated in Wundt's laboratory and inspired an important part of the programme of the new experimental psychology.

Specific Energies of the Sensory Nerves

Before the functioning of the nervous system was as well understood as it has been in the light of work in the last hundred or so years, it was assumed, partly through the corruption of a scholastic account of perception, that objects gave off a sort of image of themselves, a simulacrum, which was captured by the relevant sense organ. The elaboration of optics and the recognition of the eye as an optical device tended to confirm this view. The appearance of objects seemed to be reproduced as an image upon the retina and somehow conveyed to the sentient brain. Charles Bell maintained from his experimental evidence that the quality of the sensory experience depended upon the sensory nerves involved rather than the external event which stimulated them. For example, a blow on the eye as well as a flash of light produces a visual experience. Thus it is not a matter of some particular quality being carried along any sensory nerve whatsoever, so much as some particular sensory nerve being the carrier. In the early years of the nineteenth century this became the accepted view. However, it was Johannes Müller who put it in systematic explicit form.

Though Müller's statement of the doctrine in his *Handbuch der Physiologie des Menschen* is divided into ten laws, there are basically two major propositions. One of these is predominantly a matter of alleged physiological fact. It states that any one sensory nerve does not convey several sorts of nervous impulse but that different sensory qualities are mediated by different nerves. Several of the laws are concerned in stating this and in giving the evidence for it. The other contention is epistemological rather than physiological, although it may be thought to be required by the physiological doctrine. 'Sensation consists in the sensorium receiving through the medium of the nerves, and as a result of the action of an external cause, a knowledge of certain qualities or conditions not of external bodies, but of the nerves of sense themselves'

(1842, vol. 2, p. 1065). This is not the pure idealism of
Berkeley. It is a return to Locke. Müller maintains that
the sensation does not always parallel the object stimulating the sense organ. But even where it does he insists
upon the importance of distinguishing the external object
and the experience which it evokes.

Both parts of Müller's doctrine have been important in
the history of psychology not because they were or have
been established beyond reasonable doubt but because they
were accepted by those who shaped modern psychology in
its early phase. Errors may be as important in the history
of ideas as are truths. Both parts of the doctrine are still
controversial. There are those today who consider the
physiological hypothesis well supported by presently
available evidence but there are others, mainly working on
the skin senses, who consider it to be unsound. As we shall
see, the epistemological hypothesis is supported today only
by the phenomenalists, to be found mainly in the movement espousing cognitive theory. Phenomenalism, the belief that we apprehend not the external objects themselves
but some appearances or mental representations of them,
was built firmly into Wundtian psychology. It was challenged obliquely by James and perhaps by Külpe in his
later phase, and directly if somewhat naïvely by the
behaviourists in America, otherwise it has been accepted
by modern psychologists in a way not distinguished from
any of their other beliefs based on experimental evidence.
Indeed anyone who argues against phenomenalism except
in behaviourist company is likely to be accused of philoso-
phizing.

The physiological part of the doctrine was equally influential. Helmholtz was amongst the first to work out its
implications for particular senses. If sensory quality is less
dependent upon the stimulus than upon the sensory
mechanism stimulated, then this should apply as much
within a sense of modality as between the several modalities. It should be applicable not merely to visual quality
as distinct from auditory quality but also to the several

visual qualities. Thus began the search for primary sensory qualities. Helmholtz took up and worked out the necessary detail of the tri-receptor visual theory of Thomas Young. Even when Hering later proposed a rival theory, it did not seriously dispute the principle upon which Helmholtz based his thinking. The principle was also invoked though in less simple form when Helmholtz turned to audition. The later attempts to find primary smell and taste qualities and to break cutaneous sensitivity into its basic types were further manifestations of the influence.

At the time when the Müllerian doctrine was being formulated and extended, the volume of factual information on the senses was growing rapidly. Much of it was psychological in nature, so that experimental psychology received a rich inheritance from this source. The treatment of sensory processes in a threefold way – the sensory phenomena, the stimulus correlates and the physiological mechanisms – was firmly established in this period. The first and the second were primarily matters of observational fact, whereas the third was the focus of theorizing about the senses. The classical theories of colour vision, of hearing and of cutaneous sensitivity were concerned with the physiological mechanisms mediating the observed phenomena in given stimulus conditions.

Special attention was given to the phenomena of colour vision. Bell had noted that the several spectral colours are not equally bright phenomenally, and Fraunhofer in 1815 made the first plot of a luminosity curve. Purkinje in 1825 described the changes in phenomenal colour during the illumination changes at dawn and at dusk. He also discovered that coloured objects underwent hue and saturation changes as they were moved from central to peripheral view. Aubert in 1865 made the first thorough exploration of these zonal changes. Seebeck in 1837 concluded that there were two kinds of colour-blindness of the type described by Dalton in 1794, had Herschel in 1845 suggested that Daltonism, as it was called, was dichromatic. Colour mixture was a central topic in this period. Grassman in 1853 added his third law of colour mixture to Newton's two. The laws of intermediates and of complementaries are Newton's, at least in principle. The law of complementaries in fact awaited the insight of Grassman and the technique of Helmholtz for its demonstration. The third law added by Grassman was that colours mix in terms of their appearance rather than their physical stimulus properties. For example a seagreen of homogeneous wavelength and a seagreen obtained by mixing green and blue yield the same series of desaturated colours when mixed with red. From 1852 onward Helmholtz promulgated his elaboration of Young's tri-receptor theory. It gave an adequate explanation of colour mixture and a reasonable account of the available facts of after-images, colour contrast, colour zones and colour-blindness.

Problems of visual perception of space were also attacked with vigour. Much of the thinking here was an elaboration and refinement of principles formulated in earlier times when there were less adequate factual data. The role of convergence in depth perception had been recognized by Berkeley in the eighteenth century, and the role of the optic chiasm in the paradox of binocular viewing yielding single rather than double vision had been suggested by Galen in the second century A.D. However, the role of retinal disparity in depth perception was not understood until Wheatstone's demonstration of it in 1833, and the mechanism of accommodation was not conclusively established until Purkinje (1825) and Sanson (1838) had observed the so-called Sanson images of a flame reflected from the cornea and from the two surfaces of the lens.

Similar though not such extensive progress was made in the investigation of hearing. Savart (1831) obtained values for the lower and upper limits of hearing: his values were 16 and 24,000 cycles per second respectively. Ohm in 1843 applied the Fourier analysis of irregular periodic wave-forms to sound waves, thus resolving the problem of overtones and timbre. Beats and difference tones had been known for some time and the latter had in the mid-eighteenth-century been attributed to tone arising from beats of sufficiently high frequency. As well as producing more detailed data on difference tones of the more complex sorts, Helmholtz discovered summation tones.

The existing knowledge of vision and audition was set down and consolidated by Helmholtz in his two classics: *Handbuch der physiologischen Optik*, which was published in three parts in 1856, 1860 and 1866 respectively, and *Die Lehre von den Tonempfindungen*, which appeared in 1863. He offered in each case a theory of the sensory mechanism, endeavouring thereby to link the observed data then available on the sensory phenomena with those available on the stimulus correlates.

Little progress was made with the other senses apart from touch, where Ernst Weber (1795–1878) was the main contributor. The muscle sense had already been detached from the vaguely conceived sense of touch or feeling. Weber further distinguished the sense of touch proper, that is the sense peculiar to the skin, from general sensitivity present inside the body as well as on the skin surface. The latter includes pain, tickle and the like. Touch he held to yield three classes of sensation – pressure, temperature and location. Weber is more famous, however, for other discoveries to which we will turn later.

It is important to note that most of these observational data on sensation were so firmly embedded in the theoretical matrix of Müller's doctrine that it was regarded by the early psychologists as being as much a matter of fact as they were.

Localization of Function

A vexed question of these early times was whether the brain and nervous system worked as a single unit or as a collection of parts each with its own special function. Clinical observations guided by rather more casual impressions led the anatomist Gall (1758–1828) to a set of detailed proposals concerning localization of brain function which were wrong in every detail though correct enough in general principle. His system of phrenology rested on these erroneous localizations of function as well as on some completely gratuitous assumptions about brain development and the shape of the cranium.

It was Pierre Flourens (1794–1867) who through his careful experimental work put the principle of localized function on an adequate factual basis. His experimental technique involved the extirpation of tissue in order to establish what functions its removal obliterated or disturbed. Each set of operations and observations was guided by clearly stated hypotheses. He considered that contemporaneous anatomical knowledge of the whole nervous system justified him in taking as separate units for investigation the cerebrum, the cerebellum, the corpora quadrigemina, the medulla oblongata, the spinal cord and the peripheral nerves. His studies led him to attribute a peculiar function to each of these units. The cerebrum, he held, was essential for willing, judging, remembering and perceiving; the cerebellum for the co-ordination of the movements of locomotion; the corpora quadrigemina for seeing; the medulla oblongata was the organ of bodily conservation and mediated the transactions of what lay above and what lay below; the spinal cord had the function of conduction and the peripheral nerves that of excitation. There are some errors here of too general localization or of mislocation but they are hardly gross errors. For instance, the localization of function in the cortex is not nearly so general as Flourens thought, and only two of the four bodies of the corpora quadrigemina are involved in vision, the other two being auditory – further they are concerned in visual and auditory reflexes as well as in vision and audition.

Flourens differed from Gall not only in having better

attested localizations of function. He did not subscribe to
the fragmentation that was so central a feature in Gall's
thinking. For Flourens, not only did each major part have
its own distinctive function but also it shared in the total
functioning of the nervous system; its absence completely abolished any function specific to it, its *action
propre,* and weakened all other functions since it had
also an *action commune.* There was implicit in this treatment an acceptance of the notion of levels of functioning,
the higher levels being dependent upon the lower and in
some ways modifying them. The detailed and explicit
statement of this notion, however, had to await J. Hughlings Jackson (1835–1911) who linked the strata of neural
functioning with stages in phylogenetic evolution.

Flourens's basic studies were published in 1824 and
1825. The next important contribution to the question
of localization came from Paul Broca in 1861. Broca was
able to perform an autopsy on a patient who, despite
an intact vocal mechanism and the ability to communicate
by signs, could not speak. The autopsy revealed a lesion
in the third frontal convolution of the left cerebral hemi-
sphere – Broca's speech centre. Broca subsequently was
able to study other cases giving a general confirmation of
his conclusions. Numerous experimental studies on corti-
cal localization followed within the next two decades.
Fritsch and Hitzig in 1870 showed by electrical stimulation of the exposed cortex of a dog a fairly detailed
array of motor localization. Ferrier in 1874 made the
picture of motor localization even more detailed for the
monkey. Further, he showed that the occipital lobes were
essential in vision.

The dates here are quite important. The pendulum of
neuro-anatomical opinion had swung away from a highly
specific localization and then, just as experimental psychology was emerging as an independent study, it was
swinging back again. Thus early experimental psychology was confirmed in its fairly rigid separation of mental
functions.

Weber's and Fechner's Laws

In the course of measuring sensitivity in the various aspects of touch, Weber produced extensive but, as it turned out, far from complete evidence upon a most important relationship that had already been surmised.

In comparing objects and observing the distinction between them, we perceive not the difference between the objects but the ratio of this difference to the magnitude of the objects compared. If we are comparing by touch two weights, the one of 30 and the other of 29 half-ounces, the difference is not more easily perceived than that between weights of 30 and 29 drachms (*De tactu*, part 2, 1834; trans. E. B. Titchener in *Experimental Psychology*, vol. 2, part 2, p. 155).

He found that this ratio varied from one sense category to another. For length of lines judged by eye it was about 1 : 100, for lifted weights (i.e., judged kinaesthetically rather than tactually) 1 : 40 and for loudness of tones 1 : 160. This relationship may be expressed in more recent form as follows:

$$\frac{\Delta I}{I} = k$$

where the constant k varies from sense to sense. Just this, rather than the equation derived by Fechner from it when taken in conjunction with several assumptions about a sensory zero and sensory units, should be called Weber's law.

Fechner, a physicist of some promise, believed he could solve the relation between mind and matter by empirical, indeed experimental, means. The mind with which he was concerned was not mind-as-agent but mind-as-content, a mind consisting of phenomena such as experienced colour, sound and smell varying in intensity as well as in quality. His wish was to establish a mind-matter monism, an identity of mind and matter. To be able to show that the one was transformable in a mathematical sense into the other would be, he considered, to demonstrate this identity. Encouraged by Weber's findings he decided to concentrate upon intensity.

His *Elemente der Psychophysik*, which appeared in 1860, made a threefold contribution. On the theoretical side he added to Weber's formulation the concepts of the absolute limen as a sensory zero and the differential limen as a unit of measurement of sensory intensity. The latter of these assumptions involved treating a just noticeable difference at one point in the scale as phenomenally equivalent to a just noticeable difference at some other point. Further, Fechner assumed the additivity of just noticeable differences. With these assumptions and Weber's law Fechner derived his equation

$$S = k \log R,$$

where S is sensory intensity, k is the Weber fraction and R is the stimulus intensity above the absolute threshold. This, as Boring points out, should be called Fechner's law and not, as Fechner termed it, Weber's law. On the methodological side Fechner formulated three methods: the method of average error, the method of just noticeable differences (or of limits) and the method of right and wrong cases (or of constant stimuli). Each of these was both an experimental procedure for getting quantitative data and a numerical procedure for analysing the data. Finally, Fechner carried out a series of methodical and careful observations on lifted weights, visual brightnesses and tactual and visual distances, adding considerably to Weber's factual material.

Boring is inclined to regard this Fechnerian work as the beginning of experimental psychology. It certainly gave that subject a set of fundamental methods, it started off a technical controversy which occupied a substantial part of the early years of the subject and it gave a right to believe in the feasibility of psychological measurement. However, Fechner did not really have a psychologist's interests and may better be regarded as a benefactor than as a founder.

4 The Establishment of an Experimental Psychology of Content

It is both reasonable and appropriate to apply the adjective 'Wundtian' not only to the experimental psychology of Wundt and his immediate followers but also to the whole movement of which Wundt's thought was an expression. Helmholtz must be counted as the forerunner of this movement. Wundt himself was the principal formulator and expositor of its doctrines. Oswald Külpe (1862–1915) in his early years and Edward B. Titchener (1867–1927) in all but his last years were, after Wundt, the leading figures in a central orthodoxy. Though Hermann Ebbinghaus (1850–1901) and Georg E. Müller (1850–1934) were in no sense members of this Wundtian orthodoxy, they were with many others of less stature clearly part of the wider movement. The common aim was the establishment of an independent science which, though deriving its problems mainly from mental philosophy, undertook their investigation with experimental methods, especially as developed in sensory physiology. They believed, as Herbart had done a little earlier, that psychology could be and should be a science rather than a branch of speculative philosophy. However, unlike him, they believed that it could be an experimental rather than a formal science. It had become patent that Herbart's efforts to cope with psychological problems by mathematical analysis were sterile. By contrast, Helmholtz, in the course of his physiological work, had successfuly coped with many similar problems through the experimental method. This part of the Wundtian conviction was scarcely challenged by anyone professing to be a psychologist in the half-century following the first appearance of Wundt's *Grundzüge der physiologischen Psychologie*.

All the other features of this experimental psychology were challenged before half a century had elapsed. Quite early its particular form of phenomenalism was called into question. Thus its stress on content as contrasted with activity, its stress on sensation and sensation-like content as contrasted with more intellective conceptions of knowledge and its use of an analytic–synthetic treatment of its material as contrasted with a more holistic approach were all opposed. Later, mainly from the behaviourists, even its phenomenalism came under fire. Furthermore it was seen by differential psychology to have a deficiency in its neglect of individual differences and by medical psychology in its neglect of dynamic mental processes, especially of a subconscious kind.

Wundtian Phenomenalism

Helmholtz, in accepting the neurological aspect of Johannes Müller's theory of the specific energies of the sensory nerves, took the epistemological aspect for granted. In agreeing that the sensory experience was determined by the particular sensory neural mechanism stimulated, he assumed that the subject was aware of an appearance, a phenomenon or a representation rather than of the external object from which the stimulation originated. Nevertheless, he went beyond Müller in two ways which became characteristic of the Wundtians. First, the phenomena experienced were usually not merely the pattern of sensory impressions aroused by the stimuli. The pure sensory impression (*Perzeption,* as he termed it) was deemed to be a rare occurrence. Ordinarily it was supplemented by and given significance by images; this totality of experience constituted the *Anschauung* or perceptual presentation. In the absence of immediate sensory impressions this became a *Vorstellung* or a representative idea. Second, he held that experience built the *Anschauungen* from the *Perzeptionen.* Müller had contended that our awareness of sensory states gave us a knowledge of external objects because the former paralleled the latter through being determined by them. This was essentially a nativist view. The Wundtians followed Helmholtz in his empiristic treatment though they differed from him in the details of it. They accepted his view that perception involved two stages, namely, reception and interpretation. They did not, however, agree with him in the part he gave inference in the interpretive stage. How does kinaesthetic stimulation deriving from ocular convergence enable us to see that this object is nearer or farther than that? How does the disparateness of the binocular retinal images enable us to see some object in depth? Helmholtz believed the passage from the sensory clues to the perception was some kind of inference. Recognizing that the perceiver is conscious of neither the clues themselves nor the inference, he held the process to be unconscious. Though some notion of interpretation was characteristic of the Wundtian movement, this inferential form of it was not accepted by Wundt and his followers. Perhaps the seeming contradiction in 'unconscious inference' was a major reason for this reluctance to follow Helmholtz.

Wundt was even more explicit than Helmholtz in his statement of phenomenalism. Psychology was deemed to be concerned with direct or immediate experience as contrasted with the indirect experience in which the physical sciences found their data. The experience of a ringing bell as we hear it, irrespective of whether it be illusory or veridical, is a direct experience. The knowledge of the external world which we gain from such experience is abstracted from it. That is, some features of the direct experience are taken by themselves and regarded as apart from the experiencing subject. Knowledge of the external is then said to be mediate as it is gained through the medium of direct or immediate experience. Külpe and Titchener made this relationship of immediate experience to the experiencing subject more explicit. For instance, Titchener spoke of psychology dealing with experience from one viewpoint and physics with that same experience from another. He illustrated this with the Müller–Lyer illusion. If we consider the experience of these arrow-headed lines as dependent upon an experiencer the lines are unequal, but if we regard it as detached from an experiencer the lines are equal. Simply put, the lines are unequal 'by eye' and equal 'by footrule'. The former view is that of psychology and the latter that of physics. Though Titchener was too thorough a phenomenalist to put it thus, it may be said that the former is concerned with the way things appear subjectively whereas the latter is concerned with what they are objectively.

Elementarism

Following the implications of Müller's doctrine, Helmholtz looked for a separate neural mechanism for each basic sort of sensation within a given modality. Thus he saw the need to assume a separate mechanism not merely for visual sensation in general but also for each primary visual sensation. His knowledge of physical additive colour mixture led him to adopt Thomas Young's suggestion that there are three primary colour sensations, all others being compounded of these. This compounding is something more than the synchronous association of which James Mill spoke; it is not a mere addition of elements. John Stuart Mill had already made this point in advocating what he called a mental chemistry. Helmholtz also inherited from this associationist background the distinction between images and sensations as elements of experience.

Wundt took the first step in systematizing all this. He accepted the notion that experience was composed of elements combined in various ways. After some hesitation he settled upon three sorts of elements: sensation, images and feelings. He had at first accepted the associationist attachment of feeling, as a quality, to sensory and imaginal experience. Later he detached it and gave it independent status. Sensation and image were distinguished in terms of stimulus object present and absent. Sensation was considered to have two attributes: intensity and quality. This characterization seems also to have applied to the image. In his later theorizing Wundt proposed a tridimensional theory of feeling, in which he added to the traditional pleasure–unpleasure dimension the further dimensions excitement–calm and tension–relief.

It should be noticed that in Wundt's theory of elements there is a double elementarism. First, there are the three types of elements, none of which can be reduced to any other and second, there are the attributes whereby any instance of an element is to be distinguished from any other. Wundt detected no anomaly here. Külpe and Titchener, who both were more systematic theorists than Wundt, tidied this thinking about elements in several ways. Of primary significance was Külpe's clarification of the theoretical status of the terms 'element' and 'attribute' (1893). When some constituent of experience can occur independently of any other, it is an element: a sensation may in fact ordinarily occur with images but, at least in principle, a sensation may occur apart from any images. When some constituent of experience can vary independently of any other even though it cannot occur independently, it is an attribute: a colour cannot occur without some degree or other of brightness but colour and brightness may vary independently of each other (at least within certain ranges). Until Külpe argued to the contrary, Wundt had regarded feeling as an attribute of sensation. Külpe pointed out that sensation may be neutral, i.e. have no feeling, and that feeling itself has attributes such as intensity and quality. He concluded that feeling, like sensation, must be an element.

Külpe also added to the list of attributes. All experience, whether sensation, image or feeling, varies not only in respect of intensity and quality but also in respect of duration. Further in some modalities, notably vision and touch, both sensations and images vary also in respect of extension. Titchener in 1908 added volume, somewhat akin to extension, for sound and the attribute of clearness for all modalities. The 'volume' intended is not that meant by the manufacturer of radio receivers. It may be recognized in the difference between the 'big' tones of an organ and the 'thin' tones of a piccolo. This is not solely a matter of pitch. Clearness or attensity as an attribute is an interesting example of an attempt to treat attention strictly in terms of content. All these newly recognized attributes of the psychical elements had been regarded by Wundt as belonging solely to the compounds and thus as resultants of the combination of the constituent elements. Shifting their location in this way represented a lessened emphasis on the 'mental chemistry' of Wundt's treatment as well as some retraction from his radical empiristic allegiance.

Though Külpe and Titchener in their earlier systematizing moved along parallel paths, they ultimately diverged markedly from each other. Külpe at Würzburg inspired a series of experiments on thought beginning with Mayer and Orth (1901) and ending with Karl Bühler (1908) which seemed to call for the assumption of a fourth element, the *Bewusstheit* or the imageless thought. This was bitterly contested by the orthodox, Titchener being the principal spokesman in his *Lectures on the Experimental Psychology of the Thought-processes* (1909). There was argument too for the introduction of a variety of non-content notions such as determining tendency and set. The issues in the ensuing controversy were so tangled that varying interpretations have been placed upon it. The view urged here is that Külpe was shaking off his phenomenalism rather than adding variety to it. Though the imageless thought was referred to as another element, what is more important is that it involved the notion of cognitive reference to an object other than through a phenomenal medium. Phenomenalism had been so much tied to sensationism (images being pale copies of sensations) that its rejection seemed to need the prior assertion of sensationless (or imageless) cognition.

Titchener, on the other hand, became more deeply

sensationist. In his posthumously published *Systematic Psychology: Prolegomena* (1929) he maintained that the three elements – sensation, image and feeling – each had a sensory character. At the same time he laid less stress on the elements as the basic terms and more upon the attributes of sensory experience. This change followed a sharp controversy, conducted mainly in the United States, over which was primary – element or attribute (see Rahn, 1913). The main consideration was theoretical nicety, though some experimental evidence was also involved. Titchener turned to a position ultimately formulated by E. G. Boring in his *Physical Dimensions of Consciousness* (1933) in which it is argued that experience is best characterized in terms of independent dimensions (or attributes which are continua).

Wundtian Introspection

Though the Wundtians deemed psychology to be an experimental subject, they in no way departed from the traditional view that introspection was the form of observation to be employed. They did not, of course, rely solely upon it, being ready to use a variety of what later came to be called objective methods. Nevertheless, these procedures were ancillary to the main method. The reaction time experiment, for instance, may be carried out in a completely objective way, yet in Wundtian hands its context was strongly subjective. Detailed introspections were ordinarily obtained about the fore-period, when the subject was awaiting the signal, and about the main period, when the reaction was in progress. Likewise the objective methods employed to study the bodily accompaniments or expressions of feeling were deemed to have point only in so far as what they revealed could be correlated with what introspection uncovered. Though later behaviourists have been able to treat the psychophysical methods as objective, such a thought seems not to have occurred to the Wundtians.

The conception of introspection favoured by these early experimentalists was derived from empiricist philosophical psychology and was at variance with the more popular conception which derived from rationalist sources. In the latter view associated with act psychology, which will be examined in the next chapter, there is a clear-cut dualism: on one side are the events of the external world and on the other are the mental processes which, amongst other functions, are 'knowings' of at least some parts of the external world. Introspection is then the exercise of an inner sense enabling us to have a knowledge of these inner processes. As it has often been put, consciousness is also self-consciousness: the mind knows its own activities in its knowing the external world, and it has this self-knowledge simultaneously with its knowledge of the world. The British associationists had been at pains to combat this view. Mind for them was simply a set of sensations and ideas. Having a sensation and knowing a sensation were one and the same thing. With no mental agent ('the mind') and with no mental act there was only content to be had and to be reported. This was the line followed by the Wundtians. They admitted no valid distinction between an outer and an inner experience, arguing that there was a single sort of experience which might, however, be considered from two different points of view. It might be considered as giving information about the external world (the viewpoint of the physical sciences) or it might be considered simply for its own properties (the viewpoint of psychology).

This conception of a single experience open to a double consideration is possible within a sensationist or, even more generally, a cognitive psychology. The handling of affective states encounters some difficulty unless they are transmuted into cognitive states. In Wundt's early theorizing, feeling was an attribute of sensation. In considering experience as immediate, such an attribute had to be taken into account, whereas in abstracting from this experience information about the external world, it could be largely if not wholly ignored. When, however, feeling was elevated to the status of an element, this manoeuvre was not so easily carried out. Thus an unpleasant roughness of touch can be regarded from the two viewpoints but an unpleasant feeling of depression cannot be (though of course some cognitive component accompanying it may be). This difficulty may well have been influential in Titchener's return to the characterization of feeling as sensory, even though he preserved it as an element. The phenomenological conception of introspection deriving as it did from the 'inner experience' tradition was in a better position to handle affection. As we shall see later, the phenomenologists urged the adoption of a naïve attitude, that is, the shedding, as far as possible, of one's presuppositions and expectations. In this way it was hoped to achieve an account of experience precisely as it occurs to one. The Wundtians maintained that we are so oriented towards the external world that a deliberately adopted analytic attitude was necessary for us to notice what our experience in itself is like. Failure to recognize this resulted in what Titchener called the 'stimulus error', which is the reporting of the supposed objective stimulating conditions in mistake for the sensory experience itself. Titchener gave as one example of this error the tendency of the naïve subject, in a determination of a difference limen, to think of the several grey papers rather than of the visual sensations of several brightnesses resulting from looking at the papers. Elsewhere, he spoke of the long training required to enable the effective adoption of this analytic attitude.

Mental Composites

Helmholtz said that pure sensory impressions (*Perzeptionen*) were rare occurrences. Wundt went further in saying that 'all the contents of psychical experiences are of a composite character', the elements being 'the products of analysis and abstraction'. This notion of experience being composite and analysable into elements was a central doctrine in the whole movement. An empiristic account of the genesis of the composite experiences was generally favoured.

Wundt himself divided these composite experiences into intensive and extensive. In the former the features of the elements are merged or fused as in the mixture of two primary colours and as in the clang resultant from two pure tones. In the latter the elements are ordered in relation to each other temporally (as in a melody) or spatially (as in a drawing) or both (as in a dance). Each of these kinds of composite may be distinguished in terms of its production or origin. Some combinations of elements come about through relatively passive or mechanical associative processes, whereas others are the product of more active and selective apperception.

The notion of extensive associative combinations was a continuation of the synchronous and successive associations of James Mill and others. For Wundt they were the bases of our experience of spatial and temporal properties. The notion of intensive combinations was in accord with John Stuart Mill's contention that a mental chemistry as well as a mental mechanics was needed. Wundt recognized that in extensive associations there was an order present which was additional to the properties of the elements; some thinkers on the fringe of the movement later argued for a 'form element'. In intensive combinations there were properties, other than the general feature of arrangement, not present in the elements. The properties of the elements in this case had been synthesized, creating resultant properties. English-speaking psychologists, who have learned about Wundtianism either from Titchener, who in many ways adhered more to a mental mechanics, or from the Gestalt theorists, who stressed what they disagreed with in Wundt, are prone to forget that Wundt said that mental experience is more than the sum of its parts. He held this to be especially the case in respect of the apperceptive combinations. Few of those in the whole movement disagreed with him. The pure elementarist is largely a fiction, a caricature drawn by the opponents of Wundtiansim.

Herbart had spoken of impressions, whether sensory or ideational, emerging into consciousness over a threshold or limen of intensity. Within consciousness too such states were capable of attaining different levels of attention. All of this was not an automatic process depending upon the inherent forcefulness of the impression itself. Much depended upon its being relevant to and assimilable by the core of ideas prevailing at the time. This core was spoken of by Herbart as the 'apperceptive mass'. Wundt likewise closely linked attention and apperception. 'The state which accompanies the clear grasp of any psychical content and is characterized by a special feeling we call *attention*. The process through which any content is brought to clear comprehension we call *apperception*' (1897, p. 209). The process may be passive, as when new content by its vigour forces itself into attention, or it may be active, as when its occurrence has been prepared for by the prior presence of other relevant content. In the active form, the process is accompanied by initial feelings of expectation and by terminal feelings of fulfilment. Wundt went on to distinguish the simple apperceptive functions of relating and comparing from the complex functions of synthesis and analysis made up of varying combinations of relating and comparing. Relating is the taking together of two items of content, and comparing is the noticing of similarities or of differences in such related items. Weber's law and the growing mass of data upon it were discussed by Wundt under this rubric. The higher mental processes of imagination, understanding and conceptualization, all characterized by means of their contents, were accounted for in terms of the complex apperceptive functions.

Though the notions of elements being combined to form ordinary experience and of attention as a descriptive event remained a central part of the Wundtian psychology as a whole, this specific notion of apperception was discarded by most members of the movement. Ebbinghaus in his *Abriss der Psychologie* (1908) specifically rejected the term as being too ambiguous, though he stressed the active character of perception as an information-gaining process. Referring to the impact made by stimuli upon the sense-organs, he stated that we perceive less than is available to be perceived (that is, perception is selective), we perceive more than is available (that is, perception includes an enrichment through images derived from past experience) and we perceive the components in groups or ordered parts (that is, we perceive significant and distinct things).

Titchener treated apperception in an even more stringent way than Ebbinghaus who had preserved many of its active features. In his *Primer of Psychology* (1898) Titchener used the term to designate the process of attention, stressing selectivity. He attributed this selectivity not to any ideational apperceptive mass but to states of the nervous system. Later in his *Textbook* (1909) he rejected the term. As we have seen already, the levels of attention were regarded ultimately by Titchener as a feature of content. Selectivity was preserved but was accounted for, at least in so far as a psychological account was offered, by reference to relatively mechanical factors. The notion of imagery added to sensation was also preserved but as an associative product. Some trace of the original doctrine remained, much modified, in Titchener's context theory of meaning. The meaning of a content, according to this, consists in the contents which form a context for it: principal amongst this contextual material were kinaesthetic and verbal imagery. The inadequacy of this theory of meaning reveals an important weakness in any psychology based purely on content. Holistic phenomenalism fares no better with meaning than did Titchener's elementarism. It is important, too, to note how the orectic aspects of mind were dealt with by the Wundtian movement. Wundt himself, after the recognition of feelings as elements, applied the general principles of compounding to them. Emotions, for instance, are specific sequences of feelings with cognitive accompaniments, both sensations and images. A threefold characterization of emotions was suggested, namely in respect of quality, intensity and mode of occurrence. Thus rage was characterized as unpleasant and depressing in quality, strong in intensity and irruptive in occurrence. Emotions were deemed to have two possible modes of termination – a fading back to the normal unemotional state or a sudden change in ideational and affective content, which brings the emotion to an end. The latter change was equated with the volitional act. Motive was likewise treated in terms of phenomenal content. 'Those combinations of ideas and feelings which in our subjective consciousness are the immediate antecedents of the act (or volition), are called *motives* of volition' (1897, p. 185). In his early analysis of these processes Titchener stressed ideas of anticipation. In his later work his interest seems to have been largely withdrawn from these non-cognitive problems. Such a withdrawal was inevitable unless certain of his ruling convictions about experience were to be abandoned. Indeed, Titchener is to be recognized as demonstrating in his pure-minded way the barrenness of a great deal of Wundtianism when it is taken to its logical conclusions.

Areas of Experimentation

The emphasis in the Wundtian movement was observational rather than theoretical, which was the reverse of the situation in its main European alternative, act psychology. Though it had a pervading set of convictions and presuppositions, it was not a closely knit system. A good deal of what James said about Wundt applies to the whole position. Writing in 1887 to Stumpf, he said of Wundt: 'Cut him up like a worm, and each fragment crawls; there is no *noeud vital* in his mental medulla oblongata, so you can't kill him all at once' (Perry, 1935, vol. 2, p. 68). Not

all the fragments proved to be viable but many of them
have had a continuing sturdy life right up to the present
though Wundtianism as a whole has long since been
killed. What survived were observational rather than theo·
retical segments. Thus the more effective way of depict-
ing this movement might be to give a thorough account
of its observational work. Space precludes giving any
more than a few samples here.

In many ways Wundt's own first purely psychological
experiment was typical of what was to come as well as
being a product of the philosophical and physiological
trends, which produced this 'new' psychology. It was done
while he was *Dozent* in physiology at Heidelberg and was
reported in the early parts of his *Beiträge zur Theorie der
Sinneswahrnehmung* (1858–62). It studied the roles of
convergence and accommodation in visual depth perception. Berkeley, the philosopher, had long before this date
dealt with the problem of depth perception, assigning a
role to convergence, and the physiologists had only recently
established the mechanism of accommodation. Wundt had
his subject look through a tube at a black thread seen
against a white background and placed at several distances
between 50 and 200 centimetres from the observer. After
noting the apparent distance of the thread at one of these
points, the observer looked away while it was moved forward or backward. Upon looking again he judged whether
it had approached or receded from him. The just noticeable differences were established for both approach and
recession under conditions of both monocular and binocular vision. Binocular vision, involving convergence as
well as accommodation, yielded much smaller limens than
did monocular vision; in the latter unlike the former
there was a marked difference between limens for approach and recession, recession being the more poorly
judged. Wundt concluded that accommodation contributed to depth perception but only when the ciliary
muscles were contracted, that is when the lens was thick-
ened. His findings and conclusions were disputed later by

Hillebrand (1894), but still later workers, for example, J. W. Baird working with Titchener (1903), have supported Wundt's finding upon accommodation in depth perception.

After Wundt had established his laboratory at Leipzig, a steady stream of students passed through it; each carried out some experimental study for his doctoral dissertation. *Philosophische Studien* was started in 1881 as a publication medium for their experimental reports. When that journal ceased in 1903, about a hundred experimental papers had appeared in it, most of them origating in the Leipzig laboratory. Meanwhile the growing pressure for a publication outlet from the other German branches of the movement led Ebbinghaus to associate himself with the physiologist, Arthur König, in producing *Zeitschrift für Psychologie und Physiologie der Sinnesorgane*, which first appeared in 1890.

At Leipzig vision received the greatest attention. There were numerous studies of the psychophysics of brightness and of colour, peripheral vision, after-images, colour contrast, as well as more perceptual phenomena such as binocular vision, form and size perception, optical illusions and seen movement. Work was also done on the other senses, especially hearing and touch, on time perception and on attention. There was also an extensive series of studies on reaction time based largely on Donders' view that by complicating the task in various ways one would be able to measure the time of the various stages of cognition. Finally, there were some studies on feeling and some on association.

A few details of some of these investigations may clarify and strengthen the impression given of this brief classification of the Leipzig work. Colour contrast was studied by Kirschmann (1890) by matching with coloured papers on one colour-mixer the induced colour in an objectively grey ring on the coloured disc of another mixer. He showed that the degree of colour induction is a function of the size of the inducing field, that the effect is greatest when brightness contrast is absent and that with equal brightness of ring and disc the amount of effect is roughly proportional to the logarithm of the saturation of the inducing colour. The investigation by G. Martius (1889) of what has since been called size-constancy was the first experiment on a topic discussed by Berkeley and still very much alive today. He placed wooden rods, 20, 50 and 100 cm. long, one at a time, 50 cm. away from the observer and had him choose from among several rods at distances of 300 and 575 cm. one judged of equal length to the standard. The matches for himself as subject were as follows:

Standard at 50 cm.	Matched length at 300 cm.	at 575 cm.
20 cm.	20·6	21·7
50 cm.	53·9	57·6
100 cm.	107·7	106·6

The matched length was slightly in excess of the real length. Also, in general the excess increased with the length of standard and the distance of the variable. However, these values represented only the slightest movement towards what the law of visual angle required. The 20 cm. standard should have been matched with a variable 120 cm. long at 300 cm. and with one 230 cm. long at 575 cm. had that law been operative.

While Kirschmann's and Martius' studies illustrate the search for the ways in which the perceiver comes to see both more and less than the information contained in the stimuli presented, a series of experiments by Tischer (1883), Lorenz (1885), Starke (1886), Merkel (1889), F. Angell (1891) and Kämpfe (1893) illustrate the methodical attempt to verify Weber's law for sound intensity. In those days a wooden or metal ball was dropped on some resonant structure from various heights in order to produce sounds of various intensities. Noises so produced rather than tones were not the best stimuli for testing Weber's law. Also this crude method of controlling intensity was adequate for no more than the roughest test. Nevertheless these early workers with these crude procedures were able to show that their experimental data approximated the law. The problem, with some twists, continues to be worked upon, though with modern instrumentation the Leipzig data have now no more than historical interest. One other quantitative concern at Leipzig, though lively at the time, proved to be a fragment of the worm which had little future. Wundt took over Donders' use of the complex reaction time as a means of measuring subtractively the minimum duration of the higher processes. Complication after complication was added, the difference in mean times of the newly complicated task and the level below it was taken as the time for perception, apperception, choice or whatever it might be. From 1883 to 1892 *Philosophische Studien* reported study after study of this sort, the most famous being Lange's in 1888 which discovered the difference between 'sensorial' and 'muscular' reaction times. The conception upon which the central interest of this work was based was an example of summative elementarism at its worst. The saving comment to be made is that it was Külpe who in 1893 (and still within the orthodox fold) showed the sterility of it. Reaction time is not without its modern interest but most of this early Leipzig work must be regarded as the exploration of a blind alley.

Outside Leipzig a great deal of work from a similar viewpoint was proceeding on all these topics. Some of this was done by psychologists, G. E. Müller's work on psychophysics, both in particular sense departments and as a matter of method, being a leading example (1896). Some was done by physiologists (like König) who following Helmholtz may reasonably be counted as workers in the experimental psychology of content. Memory and the higher thought processes were not neglected as they were at Leipzig. Ebbinghaus opened up the investigation of memory, devising experimental procedures and materials such as the savings method and nonsense syllables as well

as producing a mass of evidence on memorizing and for-
getting. He published this work in his classic monograph,
Über das Gedächtnis (1885). G. E. Müller followed this
lead with a series of investigations which put the factual
and methodological sides of the psychology of memory on
as clear a footing as he provided for psychophysics. By the
beginning of the twentieth century a great deal of precise
information was available on rote memory.

The experimental investigation of thinking was undertaken by Külpe and his associates at Würzburg but
Wundt was unable to approve of it. Wundt's faith in the
experimental method did not extend so far, or perhaps
his conception of the experimental method was not so
wide. There were many points at issue here such as the
need for repetition in experiment and the need to confine
introspection to reporting what had been experienced.
Külpe was shifting from Wundtianism to phenomenology and to a psychology of mental acts, and in doing so
was straining the Wundtian conceptions of experimentation and of introspection. Wundt himself believed that
some aspects of human mental nature could only be revealed by a historical-sociological type of inquiry. For
him, his monumental *Völkerpsychologie* (published in ten
volumes between 1900 and 1920) was as important as the
monumental *Grundzüge der physiologischen Psychologie*.
But for Wundtianism, as it has been discussed here, it is
the latter which was important. Indeed in some ways, it
may be said that an equally monumental work, Titchener's *Experimental Psychology: A Manual of Laboratory Practice* in four volumes, two for the student, and
two for the instructor, published from 1901 to 1905
represents more unequivocally the true spirit of the movement.

The General, Human, Adult, Normal Mind

Titchener on at least one occasion stated that the experimental psychology which Wundt had begun was con-

cerned with the general, human, adult, normal mind.
He might have added after the word 'mind' the phrase
'conceived as content and studied analytically'. He rightly
stressed that this psychology relying as it did on introspection could properly include only the normal adult
human mind. The other animals, if they can introspect,
cannot report the results of this activity. The mentally
disturbed human being is clearly not fit to be a scientific
observer and the child is not ready to be trained in analytic observation. In the Wundtian view of science only
the general is significant – individual variations are either
to be regarded as deviations from the 'law' or to be regarded as errors and eliminated by averaging of results.
Psychology later came to distinguish the subject from the
observer and so admitted the non-human animals, the
young and the deranged amongst human beings. Evolutionary theory working through functionalism opened
the door for the animals and the young (and incidentally
the old) as subjects, and medical psychology which grew
up largely outside the traditions so far discussed admitted
the deranged. A further outside tradition which was reinforced by evolutionary theory grew into differential
psychology and contributed a scientific interest in individual variation. However before we turn to consider
these developments, we need to look at another largely
German movement which provided an alternative to the
Wundtian psychology of content.

5 Act Psychology and Early Phenomenology

The young scholar of 1874 eager to be a psychologist in the modern style was confronted with two clear alternatives in Wundt's *Grundzüge der physiologischen Psychologie* and Brentano's *Psychologie vom empirischen Standpunkte*. Wundt offered a psychology of mental content, an elementarist way of handling these contents and a mode of deciding issues which resorted more to observation than to logical analysis. By contrast, Brentano argued for but did not fully present a psychology of mental acts, was more inclined to holism than to elementarism even though he was deeply concerned with the classification of mental acts, and resorted to logical analysis rather than methodical observation even though he was more empiricist than rationalist in spirit. Wundt's philosophical background had been British empiricism coloured a little by German idealism. Brentano, who had been trained in philosophy and theology and not in physiology, was steeped in scholasticism. He was, of course, well aware of modern thought and was ready to come to grips with it. His was a more subtle mind than Wundt's as well as being a more independent one.

The roles played by Wundt and Brentano in their respective movements were quite different. Wundt was a master with a school – indeed with a school within a school for the Leipzig group formed as we have seen a central orthodoxy within a fairly homogeneous set of doctrines. Brentano, by contrast, had no school in this sense. Nevertheless he was intellectually influential: he appealed to independent minds who, though ready to follow up many of his lines of thought, were not ready to follow him. Amongst the more notable of these were Carl Stumpf (1848–1936), Theodor Lipps (1851–1914),

Oswald Külpe in his later phase and August Messer (1867–1937) in Germany, James Ward (1843–1925), G. F. Stout (1860–1944) and less directly William Mc-Dougall (1871–1938) in Britain and, in Austria, Alexius Meinong (1853–1920), Christian von Ehrenfels (1859–1932), Stephan Witasek (1870–1915) and Vittorio Benussi (1878–1927). The last group together with Brentano constituted what has been called the Austrian school; their main university locations were Vienna, Graz and Prague. Except for Stumpf, who was mainly at Berlin, the German act psychologists were located in southern Germany which, perhaps because predominantly Roman Catholic, tended to share in the Austrian modes of thought.

Brentano's relation to those who followed him was such that it makes it desirable to discuss him first. Further, we shall need to consider the phenomenology formulated under Brentano's influence by Edmund Husserl (1859–1938). Phenomenology affected many of the later act psychologists and coloured even more strongly the *Ganzheit* movement which succeeded act psychology in Europe and which later spread to America often with the adjective 'phenomenological' prefixed to its psychology.

Brentano's Neo-Scholasticism

Brentano's philosophical scholastic background exerted no strong pressure upon him to adopt either elementarism or sensationism. There was, of course, an inherent bias towards cognition, though the framework was not such that orectic processes could not be readily fitted into it.

In seeing a coloured thing or in recollecting a past event in Brentano's view, the mentality consists in the seeing and in the recalling and not at all in the coloured object as seen or in the event as recollected. Except when the object of the act is another act, it is in itself (that is apart from its being the object of an act) either physical or conceptual. The act is a reference to the object and as such it requires an object. One cannot just perceive, one perceives something; one cannot just desire, one desires something. The object as object of a psychic act does not exist apart from the act, though the physical thing or the conceptual situation as fact may. A desired object is such only so long as it is desired and a recollected one only so long as it is recollected. It may be an objective situation even if desired or recollected by no one.

Every physical phenomenon is characterized by what the scholastics of the Middle Ages have termed the intentional (or, sometimes mental) inexistence of an object, and what we (although the expressions are not wholly free from ambiguity) should term reference to a content, direction upon an object ('object' not meaning here a 'reality'), or immanent, objectivity. All alike contain within them something as their object, although they do not all contain the object in the same way (*Psychologie vom empirischen Standpunkte*, 1874, trans. E. B. Titchener, *Amer. J. Psychol.*, 1922, vol. 33, p. 43).

Brentano distinguished three classes of act, three ways in which an object may exist in an intention or may be referred to. The first was ideation or the mere presentation of the object; through it the mind non-committally apprehends the object. Sensing and imaging are instances. Acts of the other two classes presuppose this basic reference and involve it. In judging and in loving–hating, a stand towards the object is taken. In the former, it is perceived to be thus or to be otherwise, it is accepted as true or rejected as false. In the latter, it is taken as pleasing or as unpleasing, it is desired or avoided, it is accepted as right or rejected as wrong. All this, of course, is established not through careful, methodical observation but through a careful, logical analysis of what any thoughtful person knows about his mental life. The evidence for the classification is empirical but it is not the result of methodical observation. Christian von Wolff and, following him, Immanuel Kant had accepted a threefold division of mental functioning, namely cognition, affection and conation; the two latter may be thought of as a sub-division of the medieval category of *orexis* into two. Brentano in his classification recombined these two but subdivided the noetic category into ideation and judgement, a division much along the line of the old higher–lower levels cleavage. This question of the classification of the acts was one that occupied a great deal of attention in the whole act psychology movement. The other issue upon which there was a great deal of to-and-fro of opinion was whether the objects (or contents) had a physical or a psychical status.

One other feature of Brentano's position must be mentioned, namely the doctrine of inner perception. We have knowledge of the external world through our acts of ideation and judgement, and we may fall into error in this knowledge. We do not, however, have knowledge of our own acts in this way; instead our own mental acts are inwardly apprehended. In judging, in loving, in resolving or whatever the act may be, we are conscious of so doing, not by means of another act but as an inherent part of the act itself. This is the old doctrine that consciousness involves self-consciousness. In inner perception, Brentano held, we cannot be in error for 'no one can doubt whether the psychic condition he apprehends in himself *be*, and be *so*, as he apprehends it' (Quoted from James's *Principles of Psychology*, 1890, vol. 1, p. 187). This notion of an infallible or incorrigible inner perception is a puzzling one until we come to appreciate fully the doctrine of acts in which objects intentionally exist. The concept 'act' derives from the Aristotelian 'actual' as distinct from 'potential' and does not necessarily mean what 'activity' does. In remembering an event, something of which we are capable has become actual. What is remembered may not be real or true, since it may be a false recollection; what is remembered is nevertheless actual, since what we are remembering is whatever we remember. The pink elephants we hallucinate are not real, but when we are experiencing them the possibility of having such an object of thought has become actual. Further, that we have such

an impression, when indeed we do have it, is indubitable.
So runs the argument in brief.

Phenomenology

Act psychology had an affinity for phenomenology.
Therefore, a brief examination of that line of thought
will be profitable before we proceed to examine the
developments in the basic position after Brentano. As an
explicit philosophical doctrine and method, phenomenology seems to have been the creation of Husserl (1859–
1938). Many of his contentions had been put forward
previously but the systematization is his. He accepted the
broad features of Brentano's treatment of mind as intentional. However, he amended Brentano's conception of the
object, as did many of the later act psychologists. The
object as intended, Husserl maintained, was to be distinguished from the external object; it is a phenomenon
in the literal sense and is the starting point of our knowledge, whether of the external world or of our own minds.
Though we ordinarily proceed from the phenomenon to a
knowledge of external objects, the phenomenon itself is
worthy of prior scrutiny. This scrutiny must be made
without presuppositions about the meaning and origin of
experience and about its relation to reality. Consequently,
in order to make any phenomenological inquiry we must
shake off a number of expectations. It is not a matter, however, of avoiding the stimulus error by adopting an analytical attitude as the Wundtians recommended. Instead
we must adopt a somewhat naïve attitude in which we take
experience as it comes and not tease it apart in accordance
with some substantial and elementarist pre-conceptions.

Phenomenology as a methodical description of experience as it occurs was older than Husserl. The descriptions
of visual experience given by Goethe and by Purkinje are
examples of this earlier use of the method. They attempt to
depict colours as experienced in their living and lively en-
tirety, leaving incorporated in them all the impressionistic

features which have perhaps nothing corresponding precisely to them in the external objects themselves. Ewald Hering (1834–1918) also belonged to this tradition. For him, the appearance of yellow as an unmixed colour was an important ground for treating it as a primary colour; its phenomenal simplicity was not to be denied simply because it could be obtained by mixing.

Stumpf, who like Brentano had been one of Husserl's teachers, agreed with the latter in treating the content of the act and the independently existing object as separate. The content or phenomenon, he held, was the starting point for all science. The study of what was referred to through it was physical science and the study of the intending or reference was psychology. The study of phenomena in themselves, phenomenology, was an inquiry preliminary to both physics and psychology. Thus, for the Wundtians, contents were the material studied from different viewpoints by these two branches of science, for Brentano they were in the province of physics or other sciences of objective reality and for Stumpf they were the concern of a propaedeutic discipline. This was so in theory, but in fact the differences were not as great as these contentions would suggest. A great deal of the content that would interest a Wundtian found its way into Stumpf's classic *Tonpsychologie* (vol. 1, 1883, vol. 2, 1890) as psychology. Nevertheless the emphasis and flavour were different from what might be found in any Wundtian account of auditory sensation. For one thing Stumpf was less ready to reduce experienced sound to elements. One example of this is to be found in his theory of auditory consonance and dissonance. For Helmholtz consonance was a function of the number of shared tones. Middle C as heard has as its principal tone that produced by a stimulus of 256 cycles per second. Its overtones are the resultants of vibrations of 512, 1,024, 2,048, etc. A tone one octave up having as its principal tone that produced by 512 cycles per second, and as its overtones those produced by 1,024, 2,048, etc. is in perfect consonance. Dissonant tones come through the roughness of beats arising largely from the stimulus correlates of the overtones. Stumpf argued directly from the phenomenal sound itself rather than from the abstractive elements. Consonances are unitary fusions in which the components have been blended completely. He supported his argument by pointing to the fact that consonance and dissonance are in no way reduced by the suppression of overtones.

The observational work of the act psychologists was generally phenomenological. The palpability of sensation or, putting it another way, the identification of a stimulus correlate was not made a touchstone. Relational and emotive features were admitted as readily as the purely substantial. Experience was taken as a whole, as a texture, and was not unravelled into its separate threads. This characteristic emerged even within the pursuit of further 'elements' or types of content such as *Gestaltqualitäten* and imageless thought. It was explicit in Lipps's concept of empathy, a process whereby in effect we project ourselves into what we perceive. It came out even more strongly in Benussi's work on apparent visual and tactile movement and on perceptual grouping, in which resort was made to the act of 'production' giving rise to emergent features rather than to some process of adding higher elements to the simple or lower elements. Benussi's work like that of E. R. Jaensch, David Katz and Edgar Rubin, all three of whom were paradoxically at Göttingen with G. E. Müller, formed a link with the later phenomenological movement of which *Gestalttheorie* is a part. Jaensch studied apparent size varying independently of retinal image size, Katz made his revolutionary observations on the appearance of colour, distinguishing surface, volume and film colours and showing the interrelation of space and colour, and Rubin established the figure–ground distinction as well as the major phenomenal properties of figure and ground.

One effect of this phenomenological bent of act psychology was the inclusion of content (phenomenon) as well as act in the subject-matter of psychology. The content thus included was one in which the units tended to be 'objects' rather than 'sensory elements' on the cognitive side and in which non-cognitive components were present in their own right. Something of an anomaly, however, is to be found in this phenomenalism, for Brentano's own position had strong realist features. By realism, here, is meant the epistemological doctrine that the objects of our knowledge exist independently of our knowing them and that in our knowledge we know them directly. Wundtian-ism never wavered in its phenomenalism, act psychology often did. In saying that we see and hear objects rather than sensations, there is necessarily some weakening of the phenomenalist doctrine. The British philosopher, S. A. Alexander (1859–1938), obviously in the line of descent from Brentano, was perhaps the clearest early manifesta-tion of this realist tendency.

Acts, Contents and Objects

Logical considerations, reinforced by appeal to personal experience of mental operations, led different members of the movement to somewhat different views on two basic questions. The first of these concerned the classification of acts; the second concerned the psychical status of act, content (phenomenon) and object as well as the relations between these three terms. Brentano held that it was not the nature of the object but the way in which it was contained in the act that enabled the classification of acts. That view would seem to make the first of the two ques-tions the more fundamental. However, a consideration of the views on these two questions suggests that the second was theoretically prior. Brentano seems to have identified the object referred to in the act and the content of (that which existed intentionally in) the act. Meinong and Husserl emphasized the distinction between the two. They held that what is caught up in or is contained in the act is not the physical or external object and that this content is not what is intended or referred to. The external object was deemed to be referred to *through* these contents. Though they placed the object outside the psychical realm, they placed the content within it. Witasek and Stout preserved the distinction between content and object but blurred the original distinction between act and content. Act and content were treated by them as inseparable, as different aspects of the one occurrence. The act that referred to visible objects was visual because it was bound up with visual content. By implication, if not by explicit statement, the act which referred to a visible red object was also in some sense 'red-visual'; at any rate, there was a sort of reddening of consciousness in the reference to a red object. Here too the content was held to be psychical. In this respect Stumpf was one of the few to agree with Brentano in placing the content outside the psychical realm, though unlike Brentano he treated it, as we have seen, as phenomenal rather than physical. By and large the bipartite view of the subject-matter of psychology, namely act (or function) plus content, prevailed amongst the act psychologists. When they were observers rather than logical analysts, their attention was directed more to content than to act. Külpe and his group at Würzburg, von Ehrenfels, Witasek and Benussi are examples. Act psychology when strongly phenomenological was also primarily concerned with content, though not in the elementarist, sensationist sense in which the Wundtians conceived content.

What makes the question of the nature of contents and their relation to acts and to objects a prior question is that the classification of the ways in which the content is contained depends in part upon whether one regards the content as psychical, physical or neutral. Nevertheless, the Scholastic two-fold classification is always adopted as a framework. Brentano himself accepted, as we have seen, a basic mode of reference (ideation, mere presentation or simple apprehension). On top of this, and implying it, were the two 'yes–no' acts, judgement and interest (loving–hating). Stumpf preserved this division into noetic and orectic, but did not regard the act of simple apprehension as a base for both knowing and striving. Instead he conceived on each side a hierarchy of acts, the lower being caught up in or providing a base for the higher. The basic noetic function was a mere remarking or taking note of, the equivalent of Brentano's ideation; the content so regarded might be either sensory or imaginal. Next to this mere apprehension was the function of comprehension or grouping or combination in which spatial and temporal configurations occur. Superordinate to this was the function of conception or reference to universals, and finally there was judgement. There is some importance in this recognition by Stumpf that judgement implies conceptualization, especially when so many have taken perception to be judgement; on this analysis, perception also involves conceptualization. In the orectic division, Stumpf places willing at the top, seeking in an intermediate place and simple feeling at the bottom of the hierarchy. For Stumpf the orectic functions were more obviously bipolar than were the noetic functions.

A subdivision along von Wolffian lines of orexis into affection and conation was commonly made. Messer, Witasek and Stout all adopted cognition, affection and conation as their basic scheme. They also preserved an act of mere apprehension as the basis of all others. Witasek was most explicit on this, Messer least explicit and Stout variant in his emphasis. In his *Analytic Psychology* (1896), Stout had both anoetic sentience and mere apprehension. Both derived, it would seem, from Brentano's ideation. In order to adopt any of the 'yes–no' attitudes – judgement, feeling and conation – the object must be present to consciousness, that is, it must be apprehended or thought of. In anoetic sentience an external object makes an impression upon us without our remarking upon it or noticing it. In the phenomenon of 'hearing the clock stop', the ticking of the clock must have made an impression upon us even though we did not notice at the time. In apprehension the object is noticed. However, such a reference cannot occur by itself; it is the core of all the modes of reference rather than a separate mode of reference to an object. In his *Manual of Psychology* (first edition, 1898-9) the ultimate modes of being conscious of an object were knowing, feeling and striving. Feeling was deemed to be dependent upon knowing, and striving co-ordinate with it. To an extent, then, the cognitive mode or attitude had to do the work of both simple apprehension and judgement as given in the earlier treatment. However, conation was given the same fundamental status as cognition, the two being interdependent. We cannot strive for an object without knowing it, nor can we know it without being interested in it. This was a doctrine closely connected with Stout's conception of attention as conational rather than cognitional, a conception which runs through all his discussions. In the third edition of the *Manual* (1913), simple apprehension was restored as the precondition of other modes of the relation of the conscious subject to its objects. Implicit apprehension akin to, if not identical with, the sentience of the *Analytic Psychology* was included as well as explicit apprehension. At the same time affection and conation were not detached from each other quite as much as they had been in the first edition: they were treated here as the passive and active aspects respectively of the attitude or relation of interest. In his *Groundwork* (1903) Stout had tried a two-fold classification further subdivided. Cognition embraced simple apprehension and judgement; interest embraced conation and feeling. In the fourth edition of the *Manual* (1929), the ultimate modes were set down as cognition, affection and conation. However, behind these special relations was deemed to be a more general relation which they all presuppose. 'It is a precondition of the cognitive attitude, the feeling attitude, and the conative attitude, that there should be something before the mind with which they are concerned. When we wish to express the bare presence of an object to consciousness without indicating any more special relation we may speak of its presence in thought' (p. 98). Perhaps these changes in formulation were no more than changes in emphasis. Nevertheless, they do reveal some uncertainty on Stout's part about the need for an act of mere apprehension and about its cognitive character.

It is difficult to regard these contentions about the classification of acts as being strictly empirical. It is difficult to say what evidence of observation could be called upon to resolve the differences of opinion.

Form-Qualities and Thought

Wundtian psychology though elementarist and sensationist did not fail to consider a number of holistic and conceptual features of cognitive phenomena. However, it was less at ease with them than with some other features and it was prone to derive them from a sensationist basis. It was characteristic of act psychology, perhaps mainly through its phenomenological leanings, to emphasize these features.

Von Ehrenfels in 1890 made the first systematic analysis within act psychology of form-qualities (*Gestaltqualitäten*). He distinguished between temporal forms and non-temporal. Amongst the former are melodies and sequential changes such as the rising pitch heard when a vibrating wire is being pulled taut or the brightening of a glowing coal when subjected to a draught of air. Amongst the latter are tonal fusions, perceived movement and spatial patterns. In each of these, as Wundt himself was ready enough to assert, there are properties not found in the components. The distinctive quality of a melody is not to be found in any one of its notes nor the distinctive quality of a triangle in any one of its bounding lines. Von Ehrenfels argued that an additional quality was generated in the very combining of the elements. The further combination of first level combinations could yield higher level qualities. Where von Ehrenfels differed especially from the Wundtians was in regarding these form-qualities not as additional attributes but as additional contents, in fact additional elements though different from the commonly agreed upon elements in that they were not primary but derived. The test of an element was, as we have seen, that it could occur independently of any other particular component of experience. As all the notes of a melody could be changed by transposing it into another key without changing the melody, the form-quality of melody was held to meet the test. The same was said to hold for the other form-qualities. The argument was not accepted, however, in some quarters. Stumpf and Schumann maintained, citing a great deal of observational evidence, that it was sufficient in giving an account of holistic features of experience to recognize properties which were not present in the components and that the introduction of some higher level content was unnecessary. This roughly was the Wundtian position, though Stumpf advanced it as part of his act psychology. Attention, treated as an act, was deemed to have an important part by Schumann in the selection and grouping which in many cases contributed or constituted the form in sensory experience. Schumann backed his contention with an extensive array of experimental studies reported in the early years of this century.

Nor was there agreement amongst those who accepted form-qualities as a further type of content upon the manner in which these qualities were generated. Von Ehrenfels himself seems to have considered that the form-qualities were generated automatically by the combination of the foundational elements. Benussi and Witasek asserted that an act of production was involved. It was assumed by them that in mere apprehension the contents remain discrete. The grouping, patterning and fusing of these elements must therefore be the result of some subsequent act. Stout gave a somewhat similar role to attention which he deemed to select, emphasize and provide continuity. In these two accounts, unlike that put forward by von Ehrenfels, form-qualities were attributed to some working over of the data, that is, they were generated in some second process operating upon the contents yielded by a first process of apprehension. This was a view which the later Gestalt theorists rejected. For them the organization resulted from dynamic processes within the total contents (phenomena). They disagreed also with those who, like von Ehrenfels, considered the form-qualities to be further components rather than attributes of the total experience. Of their predecessors, Schumann and Stout came nearest to them, Schumann denying that form-qualities were added components and Stout pointing to the apprehension of total properties even when some of the constituent properties might not be noticed at all. Even so their several accounts of the generation of such features or properties were quite different. It is probably not accidental that Wertheimer took his doctorate under Külpe at Würzburg (1904), that Köhler and Koffka took theirs under Stumpf at Berlin (both in 1909) and that the famous study of Wertheimer on seen movement (1912) was done with Köhler and Koffka as subjects in Schumann's laboratory at Frankfurt-am-Main.

The other topic which showed a difference in interest between the Wundtians and the act psychologists was thought. Here too there was an attempt to add another type of content. Paradoxically the attempt began in the Wundtian camp and ended in a desertion to the other side. Whereas the work on form-qualities was as much reflective as observational, the work on thought had at its core a series of experiments. The main series was carried out under Külpe by Mayer and Orth (1901), Marbe (1901), Ach (1905), Watt (1905), Messer (1906), and Bühler (1907–8). Corroborative but quite independent studies came from Binet (1903, 1909, 1910) in Paris, and Woodworth (1907) in New York. An opposing series was conducted under Titchener at Cornell by Pyle (1909), Okabe (1910), Clarke (1911) and Jacobsen (1911). The two earliest Würzburg studies were aimed respectively at the classification of associations on the basis of introspective evidence rather than on logical considerations and at the characterization of judgement in psychological terms. Both came up with reports of non-sensory, non-imaginal states of consciousness (*Bewusstseinslagen*) but no clear attempt was made at first to give these impalpable contents systematic status. When this was attempted in later studies, there resulted a mass of evidence taken to point to a third cognitive element which was neither sensation nor image but something akin to intellection. Ach's and Messer's work pointed to at least two sub-divisions in this new class of thought elements, namely awareness of meaning and relation on the one hand and on the other awareness of rule, that is, the principle or method whereby one is to proceed in solving a problem. These contentions were confusing to others, if not confused in themselves, in that content ordinarily meant such palpable phenomena as sensation, image and feeling. At any rate, with no doubts about what to look for, the Cornell experimenters found an ample supply of sensory and imaginal content; especial importance was attached to kinaesthetic content. Külpe's movement away from a pure psychology of content was so gradual that it was not easy for either the Würzburg or the Cornell workers to recognize that what was being reported by the former was the cognitive reference to object (especially the less palpable features of objects) through other than a sensorial or imaginal medium. Had that been clear then it could have been seen more readily that the Cornell counter-experiments were to an extent beside the point. Perhaps their main historical value, as the matter now seems to stand, was to show to what lengths an elementarist and sensationist could go.

The other important finding of the Würzburg experiments was the determining tendency. Watt had drawn attention to the way in which thought followed lines set by the task or problem accepted. This introduced the concept of set. Ach added the concept of determining tendency, which was in effect the way the set worked. Both set and determining tendency were not components of consciousness. They were dynamically operating unconscious, though presumably psychical, mechanisms or agencies. They may be placed alongside a variety of other mechanisms of this type to be found in other act psychologists. The dispositions upon which Stout based his account of memory and in terms of which McDougall defined instinct are good examples. These mechanisms which were always defined relativistically (that is, in terms of what they do and not of what they are) were the modern equivalents of the faculties which the predecessors of act psychology had assumed. A more obvious revival of the earlier faculty concept was the factor concept in Spearman's theorizing. Spearman, whose views will be examined below, derived a great deal from the Austrian psychologists of the late nineteenth century.

Aftermath

As the early proponents of act psychology dropped out of the picture, the younger generation turned more and more from the original emphasis upon intentional acts. They veered away in one or other of two directions. In Europe, the phenomenological interest in the experien*ced* tended to swamp the early concern with the experien*cing*. Act psychology thus passed into the phenomenological, holistic psychology of which *Gestalttheorie* is an example. In Britain, the trend was towards functionalism of the American sort. Brunswik, originally of Vienna and a student of Bühler, also moved towards functionalism. Act psychology in its main phase had too great a philosophical component for it to remain an important movement in twentieth-century scientific psychology. Whatever the doubts about introspection as a reliable method of observation, there can not be much doubt that it enables its practitioner to say a great deal about 'contents' but very little about 'acts'. Thus in the long run act psychology did not replace the new elementarist psychology of content but gave rise to a newer holist psychology of content.

6 Functionalism

Functionalism was so characteristic of American psychological thought that it is tempting to label it American. However, it is important to recognize that where the scholastic influence prompting a logical resolution of basic issues is lessened and where the influence of evolutionary theory leading to a stress on the biological context of mental life is increased, act psychology merges with functionalism. In Britain, as has already been said, G. F. Stout and William McDougall illustrated this connexion; though there were fundamental similarities in their psychologies, one is better considered an act psychologist and the other a functionalist. There were many other functionalists on the eastern side of the Atlantic such as Alfred Binet in France, Edouard Claparède and later Jean Piaget in Switzerland, perhaps William Stern in Germany and later Egon Brunswik in Austria.

Though there can be no hesitation in naming William James (1842–1910) as the first American functionalist, his role in this movement differs from both that of Wundt in the elementaristic psychology of content and that of Brentano in act psychology. Wundt formulated the central doctrines of the content psychology and continued throughout the currency of the movement to be a major contributor to and the chief custodian of those doctrines. Brentano was the first deliberately and self-consciously to propose a psychology in which act replaced content as the basic concept, but the formulation of that psychology in any methodical way was the work mainly of others. James like Wundt and unlike Brentano formulated a whole psychology. Though it possessed a quite new flavour it was almost an unintended foretaste of functionalism. It provided much of the material and framework for functionalism, though almost equally important constituents derived from Darwinian evolutionary theory had to be blended with it. A subsidiary but important influence came from social theory, also mainly British in origin.

The role of James in the functionalist movement was more like that of Helmholtz in the elementarist psychology of content. Functionalism when it came to full strength, however, was too loosely structured a movement, too accommodating to diverse currents to provide for a counterpart to Wundt. The forerunner in these circumstances could not be succeeded by a single prophet.

The Formative Doctrines of James

In the long run, the run which converted functionalism into behaviourism, James' critical, indeed iconoclastic, attitudes were more important than any of his positive doctrines. In the short run, however, the reverse was the case. The questioning of accepted opinions was characteristic of him from the outset of his career, but in the main it was later in that career that he questioned the more fundamental traditions. Functionalism was already flowering when in 1904 he wrote his paper, 'Does consciousness exist?' which expounds the lines of thought which contributed to the emergence of behaviourism. It was the *Principles of Psychology*, written a little over a decade earlier, that was important for functionalism. He was at that time criticizing a great deal of the newly established Wundtian movement. Ridicule was used as freely for this purpose as were argument and observed fact. For example having discussed Fechner's ideas, of which so much was being made by the Wundtians, James wrote:

Fechner himself indeed was a German *Gelehrter* of the ideal type, at once simple and shrewd, a mystic and an experimentalist, homely and daring, and as loyal to facts as to his theories. But it would be terrible if even such a dear old man as this could saddle our Science forever with his patient whimsies and, in a world so full of more nutritious objects of attention, compel all future students to plough through the difficulties, not only of his own works, but of the still drier ones written in his refutation (*Principles*, 1890, vol. 1, p. 549).

We have already noted his view, tartly expressed to Stumpf, that Wundt's theorizing lacked any central doctrine from which its more restricted propositions depended. In some ways this is an odd complaint by a professed empiricist. James himself has since been said to have been no systematist and to have harboured at the one time ill-matched, indeed contradictory, views. It is true that he had difficulty in finding a stable position in the field of conflict between mechanism and voluntarism – a matter upon which something further will be said. He accepted as a general principle that mind is dependent upon brain and in his discussion of most topics he abided by this. Yet he accepted too the apparent implications of the reported findings of the psychical researchers. But perhaps he was here being less loyal to his theories than to the facts as he saw them.

Notwithstanding such incongruities, his psychology had a unity of temper and attitude. Just as his philosophy was permeated by his radical empiricism, which embraced the twin doctrines of pluralism and pragmatism, so his psychology was held together by his insistence upon viewing mind in action. 'The pursuance of future ends and the choice of means for their attainment are thus the mark and criterion of the presence of mentality in a phenomenon' (*Principles*, 1890, vol. 1, p. 8). In his discussion of habit where his mechanistic convictions were uppermost, the part played by habit in keeping mental life on an even course was stressed. In his discussion of will where those convictions were considerably undermined, he was predominantly concerned with the ways in which the person dealt with the unaccustomed and the difficult, with the situation where precedent and stock ways were not enough to guide him. Though there may be some logical incompatibilities in the two discussions they are nevertheless of a piece in that they show the ways in which mind copes with its surroundings shaping them as well as being shaped by them in the pursuit of its objectives.

Mind for James was neither agent, as it was for so many rationalists, nor content, as it was for the associationists. Yet in distinguishing his conception from each of these there is a danger of suggesting it to be akin to the other. He considered a mind to be a stream of thoughts, a term he used to cover both cognitive and orectic processes. These thoughts or occurrences of thinking were distinguished both from the brain processes which enabled them and from the objects to which they were cognitively or emotionally related. In theories of mind as agent, thinking is done by the mind. It would not be quite correct to suppose that James substituted brain states for such a mental agent, but with brain processes to bear them there seemed to him to be no need for a mind to think them. In associationist theories thoughts are what are thought about, that is, what is sensed, what is felt. But in James' view, one's thoughts were about the objects with which those thoughts were related. However James' conception of the nature of thought is difficult to pin down. Treating thought as a term related in one way to brain process and in another way to objects may have been redundant. It may have sufficed to have regarded thought as the cognitive and emotional relations which hold between brain processes and objects. Instead of having said that mind knows and welcomes or rejects objects, James might have done better by having said that mind is the knowing and welcoming or rejecting of objects, a view which is central to act psychology.

James made himself clearer upon the question of the way thought goes on. Indeed his statement of five important characters of this process was the epitome of much of his psychology.

(1)   Every thought tends to be part of a personal consciousness.

(2) Within each personal consciousness thought is always changing.

(3) Within each personal consciousness thought is sensibly continuous.

(4) It always appears to deal with objects independent of itself.

(5) It is interested in some parts of these objects to the exclusion of others, and welcomes or rejects – *chooses* from among them, in a word – all the while (*Principles*, 1890, vol. 1, p. 225).

In this characterization of the stream of thought he insisted in a simple factual way upon the 'my-ness' of mental life – an impression which some wish to blow up into a transcendental self and which others decide to ignore. He rejected an atomistic view of mind as so many substantial sensations and feelings added or even blended together. He rejected, though his immediate successors failed to appreciate this, the phenomenalist view that we are directly aware only of our phenomena (sensations, feelings). Finally, in accordance with this rejection of phenomenalism, he treated attention as the emphasis we place upon things or aspects of things in our dealings with them rather than as a competition between our various thoughts. This orientation of mental life to the real world was ultimately of great importance in the history of functionalism. However, its effect was not immediate; perhaps it had to await the reinforcement coming from evolutionary theory.

The Influence of Darwinism

The Origin of Species (1859) was addressed to a specifically biological problem, yet the solution it proposed was so radical that the acceptance of it affected attitudes towards a great variety of other issues. The account of creation in *Genesis* had led to a belief in the immutability of the animal species. Their basic similarities among their differences were attributed to their having a common creator. Darwin, though not the first to do so, contended that the various animal types underwent change over a long series of generations and that the similarities of structure and function were to be interpreted in terms of biological kinship. This contention is merely that evolution has occurred: the manner or mechanism of its occurrence is a further issue. Darwin's proposed mechanism involved natural variation, natural selection and inheritance. Any living type consists of members varying slightly one from another. These variations were deemed to be inheritable. Some of the variant features were assumed to enable their possessors to cope the better with their environments. Thus their chances of survival would be increased as would the chances of their reproducing themselves and passing on these useful features. Not only whole organisms but also particular organs such as the eye and the hand were thought to evolve and to do so by means of this triadic mechanism. Once these general ideas were accepted it became possible to arrange the whole of the animal kingdom in a great branching family tree with man not detached from the rest but occupying a place at the tip of the topmost branch.

The most general significance of the Darwinian theory was its demonstration that the 'design of creation' could have come about in a deterministic way and was amenable to deterministic explanation. This was a bitter pill for the traditionalists and thus it was important for them to point out that at best this was only an hypothesis and an unproved one – at worst it was for many of them sheer blasphemy. Darwin himself seemed to have appreciated that he must amass rather more evidence than might normally have been thought sufficient to justify the publication of the theory. As a consequence he deferred its publication to the point where he could well have been anticipated by others less patient in rounding out the story. It was fortunate that Wallace, who was one such, should have asked Darwin to present his less well-documented account, thus giving Darwin the chance to tell his own story at the same time. Though it was still only a well-supported hypothesis, it was a much better supported hypothesis than its traditional rival in the field, an explanation solely in terms of extrinsic teleology. Though, after a bitter struggle, his theory broke the long standing monopoly held by the *Genesis* story, its deterministic explanation was nevertheless given in many quarters a partially teleological interpretation. The theory itself had drawn attention to the biological consequences of particular structures and processes in relation to organismic survival. It seemed to some only a slight shift to begin thinking of the structure or process having the function of securing that consequence. Instead of the organismic feature explaining the survival, the survival was used to account for the feature.

The Darwinian account of evolution through natural variation, selection and inheritance could readily be thought of as the adaptation of animal types to the requirements of particular environments. With a slight extension, the struggle for survival could be regarded not as something in which the animal was just a pawn but as a contest in which the animal was an active participant. In some rather limited circumstances, the domineering, pugnacious animal which had the physical prowess to back its challenge might well be successful in the struggle, but in a changing and multifarious world, the flexible, the intelligent and the persistent animal would be the better equipped. This line of thought gives considerable emphasis to behavioural as distinct from constitutional assets. Darwin himself, being a field observer and not a laboratory experimentalist, was as interested in what animals did as in their structure. So he attached significance to appropriate instinctive behaviour as a contributor to survival. Vestigial instincts, that is innate patterns of behaviour which in earlier circumstances had been relevant for survival but which now were useless, were as good evidence for evolution as vestigial organs. Even more important than instinct in survival was malleability or educability of response. Lacking the later genetic concepts, especially that of mutation, Darwin was hard put to give any intelligible account of the way in which natural variations occurred. He turned as a result to the now discredited belief that acquisitions through experience in the lifetime of one organism might be passed on as a biological heritage to the next generation. The learning process was therefore seen as having a very special significance.

Darwin's *Expression of the Emotions in Man and Animal* (1872) was a clear demonstration of the value of such notions as the continuity of man with the other animals and as the vestigial retention of once useful behaviour patterns. With the aid of them Darwin was able to throw light upon some of the less rational features of human behaviour. Here was the beginning and the justification of comparative psychology. Almost at once, G. T. Romanes began to build upon these foundations with a series of studies on mental evolution. However, he outran both his resources of factual data and his resources of data-gathering technique. He was forced to indulge in a good deal of speculation based upon rather dubious anecdotal lore of animal exploits. C. Lloyd Morgan (1852–1936) in correcting these excesses was able to build more durably upon Darwin's foundations. His recognition of the need for more reliable data led him to embark on numerous simple field experiments as well as on systematic field observation. Moreover, he placed a curb upon the tendency to anthropomorphism with his law of parsimony. The way in which he formulated this variant of Occam's razor shows the extent to which evolutionary thinking had become entrenched by the eighteen nineties. 'In no case may we interpret an action as the outcome of the exercise of a higher psychical faculty, if it can be interpreted as the outcome of the exercise of one which stands lower in the psychological scale' (*Introduction to Comparative Psychology*, 1894, p. 53). The scale which Morgan had in mind was not so much the old hierarchy of faculties, the higher and lower levels of mental functioning so attractive to the rationalists, as the series of levels in an evolutionary scale. The two notions, nevertheless, are similar enough for others to be tempted to combine them.

There was a great deal in this whole evolutionary movement to supplement and reinforce the Jamesian stress on mind in purposive action upon objects in the world around it. The very notion of function came from this source. In its adaptation to the environment the organism underwent both bodily and mental changes. The task of the psychologist came to be regarded as giving an account of the roles played by mental processes in the whole process of adaptation as well as of the factors affecting the mental aspects of the adaptation. The more mechanical physiological processes were thought of as providing a means of dealing with the recurrent demands of the environment whereas the flexible and foresightful conscious processes extended the organism's capacity to deal with the variable, the novel and the unforeseen. It was here that James's more purposive notions gained strength. Oddly the influence of evolutionary theory upon psychology in the short run served to highlight conscious processes in the total functioning of the organism, whereas in the long run it led to a decreasing emphasis upon consciousness in favour of overt behaviour. The short run influence paralleled its early encouragement of a teleological mode of thought which was at variance with its basic deterministic argument.

One other influence must be mentioned here, though it will be dealt with at length in a later chapter. The Darwinian stress upon natural variation led to a concern with individual differences. Darwin's cousin Francis Galton played a leading part in developing techniques for the study of individual differences and in initiating empirical work on a wide range of bodily and mental characteristics in which people differ from one another. Such work became a dominant element in functionalist psychology.

Social Theory

Tracing the origins of late nineteenth-century social theory would take this discussion too far afield. Suffice it to say that there was a long tradition of British and French social and political theorizing in which Hobbes, Locke and Rousseau were early contributors. It was profoundly affected by the French Revolution and the British industrial revolution. In the early years of the nineteenth century it manifested itself in Bentham's radical utilitarianism with its inquiry of every social institution 'what is the use of it?' Largely from this source flowed Owen's zeal in industrial social reform and a steady procession of political reforms in Britain. In the third quarter of the century Herbert Spencer in his attempt to construct a synoptic philosophy on a grand scale linked this tradition of radical social theory with the new evolutionary thought.

There had, from quite early times, been speculation about man in primitive society but it was only in the latter half of the nineteenth century that this was provided with a reasonable empirical basis. This set anthropology on its modern course but it also generated a social psychology in that psychological concepts were introduced in order to elucidate social life. Tarde and later Le Bon were early social psychologists whose origins were in this tradition but outside the lines of thought leading to modern experimental psychology. Their discussion of the roles of imitation and suggestion in social interaction was influential for the emerging functionalism. Baldwin in America and McDougall in Britain owed considerable debts to this biologized social theory which Spencer bequeathed to the early sociologists and social psychologists.

The Establishment of American Functionalism

American functionalism emerged from a formative stage, ending in the first decade of the twentieth century, into a

self-consciously formulated doctrine. J. R. Angell (1869–
1949) was prompted by the attacks of Titchener to set out
in 1907 the main tenets of functional psychology. As he
said they were not wholly new. Indeed, much of what he
had to say was to be found in the work of other Americans
such as James, G. T. Ladd (1842–1921), G. Stanley Hall
(1844–1924), J. McK. Cattell (1860–1944), J. M. Baldwin
(1861–1934) and John Dewey (1859–1952). Though occupying distinguishable positions, these early American
functionalists had much common ground. They were all
empiricists in that they were ardently committed to the
view that psychological questions were to be answered by
facts of observation. Nevertheless apart from Hall and
Cattell they were not active observers themselves. Hall
carried out pioneering work on adolescence using questionnaires and diary methods and Cattell, following Galton, was an early worker with mental tests. All of them,
however, encouraged data-gathering through their
establishment of laboratories and their building up of
graduate schools for the training of psychologists. In this
they agreed with Wundt. Like him, they too were influenced by British empiricism and saw the importance of
linking psychology with biology. However they were
drawn more to the field form of biology than to the laboratory form. Later functionalism was also drawn to medical
biology.

Putting mind in a biological setting, especially at the
time when evolutionary theory was transforming biology,
these early functionalists were as much concerned with the
roles and the consequences of mental states as with their
kinds, combinations and trains of succession. That is, they
were as much concerned with asking 'how?' and 'why?'
as with asking 'what?'. This emphasis was reinforced by
the pragmatic philosophy which some of them were developing. James may be regarded as the co-founder with
G. S. Peirce of pragmatism. Dewey's instrumentalism was
a later variant, a pragmatism with a sociological twist.
Pragmatism was a naturalistic philosophy. It was not a

metaphysical system but a set of attitudes focused on ordinary human experience rather than on the eternal verities. For instance, the pragmatic test of a theory lay in the relevance of the theory for experience and action. The question was 'does it work?' Again, neat logical distinctions were not regarded as being significant unless they implied differences in the observed facts – a difference which makes no difference is no difference, as Peirce put it. Similarly the worth of a moral principle was to be assessed by considering its relevance to man's well-being. In this spirit, attention was given to the roles played by events, by institutions and by men, and to the consequences flowing from their operating in these ways. There was less interest in what these objects were in themselves.

Man tended to be regarded not merely as an object. Following the Scottish philosophers who had a great influence on late nineteenth-century American thought, the early functionalist saw man also as a subject. As we have already seen, James emphasized that consciousness was personal. There were not merely sensations, images and concepts or not merely sensings, imagings and conceivings. These belonged to some person, some self which possessed its own identity and continuity. Baldwin, in particular, was concerned to show how recognition of self-hood had a social origin. This concern with self was not peculiar to American functionalism. It was equally strong in British and European functionalism. For example, McDougall set out to show that self emerged through the integration, partly under social conditioning, of the innate instincts first into sentiments and later through the emergence of the self-regarding sentiment as a dominant member of the system of sentiments. An emphasis on self had been characteristic of the British act psychologists such as Ward and Stout, the latter a strong influence on McDougall. Related to this emphasis on self was a tendency to regard mental life and mental processes holistically. Stern's psychology stressed purpose, self and wholes as central concepts.

The concept of adjustment which had its origin in evolutionary thought was commonly employed. Man was seen as changing himself or changing his environment in order that he could meet its demands the better or that it meet his needs the better. This, of course, was a central notion in Dewey's instrumentalism. Thus an optimistic, progressive view of human nature and society was engendered. It was thought not merely that man and society are capable of improvement but also that anyone trying to effect this improvement is working with Nature, is aiding and hastening man's evolution. Psychology was seen as having an important contribution to make in this process. A touchingly naïve expression of this optimistic practicalism is to be found in an early passage in Ladd's *Primer of Psychology* (1894):

The practical benefits of psychology in influencing the science and art of education, the management of child-life, the instruction of idiots, the improvement of the vicious criminal and insane are becoming more clearly recognized with every year of its present rapid advances (p. 15).

Child and educational psychology were launched in this period for these practical purposes. Though the main influence from medical psychology came a little later from continental Europe, the study of abnormality was encouraged. Industrial and vocational psychology were begun, although nothing effective resulted until the mental test movement gathered greater momentum. Finally social psychology conceived with a reformist aim was encouraged. If psychology were to count it had to be shown to be capable of making a difference in man's adjustment to his environment.

Angell summed much of this up in saying

... We have to consider (1) functionalism conceived as the psychology of mental operations in contrast to the psychology of mental elements ... We have (2) the functionalism which deals with the problem of mind as primarily engaged in mediating between the environment and the needs of the organism. This is the psychology of the fundamental utilities of consciousness; (3) and lastly we have functionalism described as … the psychology which constantly recognizes and insists upon the essential significance of the mind–body relationship for any just and comprehensive appreciation of mental life itself ('The province of functional psychology', *Psychol. Rev.*, 1907, vol. 14, pp. 61–91).

The word 'function' came to be widely used, with an equally wide variety of meanings. The term could mean an operation such as perceiving as distinct from the content perceived; it could mean the role played by an operation or a content in the wider process of adjustment; it could mean the contingent relation which the operation or content entered into with the circumstances which conditioned it; and it could mean a concern with the bearing of mental processes and characters on the practical affairs of life.

The Denouement of Functionalism

A movement incorporating such diversity, if not patent inconsistency, was bound to break apart as it developed its various components. Ironically the pieces of this worm crawled off to their separate existences more vigorously and each bearing more strikingly the marks of their origin than did those originating in Wundtian psychology. Further most of them acted as though they contained the genuine *noeud vital* of functionalism.

There were first of all a numerous set of fragments devoted to the promotion of the utility of psychology. Absorbing nutriment from other sources they devoted themselves severally to serve the well-being of mankind in the family, in school, in work and in inter-personal relations. Child guidance, educational and vocational counselling, industrial psychology and clinical psychology in its various forms were all promoted within the functionalist framework of thought. They were affected to varying degrees by ideas contributed by differential and medical psychology. At the same time all bore the stamp of instrumentalism, of the concern with man's adjustment to the demands of his environment conceived in predominantly social terms. They bore the strong empiricist imprint typical of functionalism and based their practices in large measure on technically developed research. In this way they fostered the study of child development in its many facets, of individual differences for which an extensive array of tests, questionnaires and rating scales were constructed and subjected to statistical analysis, of perceptual and motor skills and of work methods, and of aberrant behaviour such as delinquency, mental disorder and ill-adjusted personal relations.

In respect of theoretical orientation a full spectrum of functionalist colours was provided, in which neighbours shaded imperceptibly into each other with opposites further down the line. At one end of this spectrum was a dynamic-personalist band usually highly receptive to ideas derived from medical psychology and given to speculative thinking. It centred on concepts such as purpose, self, values and beliefs and displayed a disinclination to adopt deterministic, nomothetic modes of thought. The influence of the Scottish school of Reid and Stewart still manifest in James tended to emerge more strongly in the thinking of American psychologists like Mary Calkins (1863–1930) and later Gordon Allport (1897–1967). Calkins thought of herself as a self-psychologist rather than as a functionalist. Psychology for her was not simply the science of consciousness but rather the science of the self as conscious. This led her, of course, to stress the self in action. In a way her psychology was an elaboration of James' view that thought tends to be personal. Allport being later is more clearly functionalist and places man more definitely in a social and biological setting. Nevertheless he too insists on the centrality of the concepts of self and person, adding that 'individuality is a prime characteristic of human nature'. William McDougall (1871–1938) in Britain and later in America and William Stern (1871–1938) in Germany adopted similar positions.

They, like Allport and others among the later American personalists, stressed human development. McDougall especially stressed self-determination as distinct from external determinism. He regarded purpose as a basic feature of all animal behaviour and self as a distinctive central component of human character. His concept of sentiment emphasized the importance of objects, ideas and situations, as valued by the person, in the guidance of his behaviour. In this he influenced Allport. In emphasizing the role of external circumstances as perceived and felt by the person, rather than as they are in themselves, functionalists in this band have increasingly come under the influence of phenomenological thinking. This was a marked feature of Stern's thought.

Nearby, indeed overlapping the more socially minded personalists, was a band concentrating on man as a *socius*. As we have seen, Hall pioneered the study of adolescence and Baldwin insisted on social factors in the development of the person. Both in America and in Britain the functionalist concern with growth spread over the full span of human life. Infancy, childhood, adolescence and senescence received prime attention, though man in maturity was not neglected. Concepts such as attitude, stereotypes and social distance, defined largely in operational terms, were formulated and developmental schedules compiled. On the left wing, as it were, of this band there was a tendency towards somewhat a-theoretical fact-gathering. The establishment of norms and the correlation of this with that was common. Indeed on this side the band shaded into a similarly positivist band of experimentalists, devoted to the study of sensory discrimination, verbal learning, acquisition of skill and the like. We have here in these neighbouring bands the field and the laboratory workers of positivist temper. Together they constituted what was sometimes referred to in America as 'dust-bowl empiricism' as they flourished in the Mid-West. They also provided the complementary functionalist colour for the first described group of personalists, for they contrasted not only in respect of their attitude to theorizing but also in their stress on the overt and the objectively specifiable. Those on the right wing of the socio-development band were not confined to America but were to be found in Britain and on the European continent as well. Alfred Binet in France and later Jean Piaget in Switzerland, and overlapping them in time C. W. Valentine in Britain, were amongst those who have contributed to our knowledge of development during childhood. Those more concerned with socialization and social interaction tended to join with the sociologists who had similar interests. Though the earlier functionalists studying man as a social animal made much use of the concept of instinct as developed in evolutionary biology, the sociological affiliations of the later members were mainly responsible for the onslaught on that concept. There was a corresponding swing away from hereditarian to environmentalist thinking on other topics considered by them. The emphasis on learning by the early functionalists was strengthened in this band.

At the other end of the spectrum from the personalists was a biotropic band, mainly laboratory workers willing to theorize but chary of wide ranging speculation and of what seemed to them to be vague concepts. The Columbia functionalism of E. L. Thorndike (1874–1949) and R. S. Woodworth (1869–1962) was in this band. Its theories tended to be close to the factual ground and were meant to illuminate some modest range of facts such as problem-solving by animals and men (Thorndike's trial-and-error theory of learning derived from Alexander Bain, the last great British associationist), transfer of learning (Thorndike and Woodworth's theory of common elements), the role of inner conditions in determining the direction of association and the form of perception (Woodworth's notion of mental set) and so on. They favoured an S–R formulation of psychological problems, providing both innate and acquired linkages between stimuli and responses. Though inclined to concentrate on objective observation and on observed variables, they were ready to be flexible in applying the terms 'stimulus' and 'response' and in allowing for intra-organismic determinants. Mental set was one of the latter, drive and satisfaction were others. Woodworth came to argue that the basic formulation should be S–O–R rather than the seemingly empty organism view expressed in S–R. Woodworth in his *Dynamic Psychology* (1918) made the important distinction between response mechanism and drive and went on to explore the physiological bases of drive (recognizing at the same time but not delineating the role of social factors). One may think of this band of functionalists as liberal behaviourists.

Readers concerned about the non-spectral purples in the array of functionalist colours may find them in linkages between the dynamic psychology of Woodworth and his kind and the dynamic psychology of the personalities. At an early stage the concept of instinct provided one link, but the more general form of this link is provided in the stress on inner determinants of behaviour. The S–O–R theorists gave a more mundane, a more biological account of these determinants whereas the personalists were more ready to resort to vaguer and at times more mystical conceptions. The former stood more firmly for determinism and for the view that psychology is a law-seeking science. The general biological flavour in both and the 'inward' emphasis provides a complementary colour to the environmentalism and the 'outward' emphasis in the green region of the sociological band of functionalism.

Whereas Titchener had been able to say that the science of psychology was concerned with the generalized, adult, normal, human mind, functionalism reinforced by differential and medical psychology found places for the individual, the child, the adolescent, the senescent, the abnormal (socially, emotionally and intellectually) and the animal mind. There were trends in it tending to ignore even the mind, trends which later manifested themselves in behaviourism.

7 The Incorporation of Differential Psychology

Though the functionalist concern with individual differences has already been mentioned, it is important to recognize that attempts to depict and to account for differences amongst individuals made prior to the late nineteenth century occurred almost entirely outside the main lines of thought which led to the foundation of general scientific psychology. The interest in individual differences was, however, persistent and of very ancient origin. There had been three traditional ways in which this interest had expressed itself in dealing with temperament. The first, with which the name of Theophrastos is associated, consists of literary sketches of distinctive characters. In his work *Characters*, Theophrastos gave a series of thumb-nail sketches of types such as the avaricious man, the gross man, the flatterer and the garrulous man. Each is marked by a dominant trait which manifests itself in various attitudes and behaviour. In post-Renaissance times this literary genre attracted many practitioners in Britain and France. It also was adopted in more complex form in those comedies in which different types are placed in a situation which fosters their interaction. The second tradition is illustrated in Galen's classification of temperaments. Hippocrates in accord with the doctrines of four basic properties – hot, cold, moist and dry – and of the four basic elements – earth, water, air and fire – maintained that there were four basic fluids or humours in the body, namely blood, phlegm, yellow bile (Greek *khole*) and black bile (Greek *melas*, black + *khole*). Galen asserted that a predominance of one humour over the others produced a distinctive temperament. Thus the sanguine (Latin *sanguis*, blood) person is optimistic, emotionally shallow and with outwardly turned interests; the phlegmatic person is stolid, insensitive, slow to be aroused though obstinate; the choleric person is irascible, impulsive, prone to dominate others and subject to violent if short-lived emotion; and the melancholic person is inwardly turned, contemplative, depressed and inhibited. These together with some admixtures constituted Galen's classification of temperaments. Whereas the set of characters of Theophrastos is open, Galen's system of temperaments is comprehensive. Having depicted a score or even a hundred characters each with his distinctive trait, it is always possible to think of some others. On the other hand granted Galen's basic determinant of temperament, namely the predominance of one of a limited set of humours, the system is complete. Most medically based typologies of recent times, such as those of Jung, Kretschmer and Sheldon, share this feature with Galen's. The third tradition had an early manifestation in *Physiognomica*, a work dubiously attributed to Aristotle. In it temperament is said to make itself apparent in the face. Predominant moods such as cheerfulness or despair were thought to leave their marks in the set of the face. Further, resemblances to the lower animals were deemed to be signs of traits characteristic of those animals. Thus a fox-like face was held to betoken cunning whereas a bovine face to betoken stolid placidity. Phrenology, graphology and the like are extensions of this tradition. At somewhat greater remove are the correlations between temperament and physique such as proposed by Kretschmer and Sheldon.

In early modern times these traditions became inextricably mixed. For instance, the title of Ben Jonson's *Every Man in his Humour* proclaims some allegiance to Galen. Each member of its *dramatis personae* had his central dominating trait and in the anglicized version each bore a name appropriate to his character – Knowell, Brainworm, Downright, Wellbred, Cash, Clement and Formal. No doubt in the production each had a mien, deportment and dress to match.

Galton's Substitution of a Scientific Approach

A more productive alternative to such pre-scientific approaches was first provided by Francis Galton (1822–1911). Though four main contributions made by him need to be considered here, these by no means exhaust his many contributions to modern science.

Foremost amongst his contributions to differential psychology were his substitution of a quantitative for the earlier qualitative approaches and, associated with this, his application and extension of statistical methods. He was impressed by the finding of the Belgian mathematician Quetelet in 1846 that the chest circumferences of a number of Scottish soldiers were distributed approximately in accordance with the Gaussian curve of error or as we now so often call it the normal distribution. In his examination (1869) of the marks awarded in mathematics at Cambridge Galton recognized that he had the upper end of a similar distribution. He went on to gather data on various features of living organisms such as length of leaves on plants and memory span in man in order to convince himself that comparable variations in degree were general. Thus he substituted for the conception of individual differences as discrete qualitative types the conception of them as constituting quantitative continua with a typical form of distribution.

In order to demonstrate this as a matter of fact he collected a great deal of anthropometric data. In order to extend his survey into the psychological field he devised several instruments for the better measurement of sensory discrimination and formulated tasks calling on other functions in a way which yielded measures. These were the first mental tests, though the name was given them a little later by James McKeen Cattell. To show the form of the distribution of individual variations Galton used what we now call the frequency distribution table. Over and over again he showed the high density of instances in the middle region with a characteristic pattern of decrement in instances deviating on either side of this central tendency. In order to compare two samples in respect of the same characteristic he computed the median as an index of central tendency and the quartile deviation (semi-interquartile range) as an index of dispersion. Further when he wished to compare variation in different characteristics he converted the original measures into deviations from the median in quartile deviation units. Though in detail his methods were often crude, in principle they have a completely modern flavour. This is perhaps best illustrated by his introduction of the correlation method (1888), a method put into better mathematical form by his protégé Karl Pearson at the end of the century. All the basic ideas, however, were Galton's – the correlation table, the concept of regression towards the mean, the two lines of regression and the correlation coefficient (or index of co-relation as he called it). Even the symbol r was his.

Almost equally influential as these three abiding contributions – the quantitative conception of individual differences, mental tests and the use of statistical methods – was his deep-seated conviction that individual variations were basically innate and inherited. Though unaware, in common with his contemporaries, of Mendel's formative discoveries upon which modern genetics is founded, his examination of the data available to him led him to conclude that inheritance is essentially particulate. He believed that human abilities, as well as physical traits such as stature, were so inherited. His data were of two sorts: family trees or pedigrees and correlations between parents and offspring. They showed that men of outstanding ability were more likely than others to have distinguished parents, distinguished offspring and distinguished relatives. They also showed what seemed to Galton to be a law of nature, though it is a mathematical consequence of the situations with which he was working, that outstanding men have sons who on the average are less able than their fathers and that men of low ability have sons who are on the average more able than their fathers. He spoke of this as a law of regression to mediocrity whereby a group of living organisms was kept in equilibrium through the generations. Of course the law holds 'up' the generations as well as 'down' them and is the consequence of their being steady.

By the early years of the twentieth century many pedigrees were collected by numerous workers. One of the most widely cited was that produced by Goddard on the descendants of an American Civil War soldier whom he named Martin Kallikak (from the Greek words *kallos*, beauty and *kakos*, evil). It is odd that the two women from whom the fair and the foul lines respectively descended were given the credit and the blame for Martin's two lines while he was allowed to stand aloof exempt from both. This like Galton's pedigree studies had no way of disentangling environmental and hereditary influences. Without doubt all these studies under-estimated the role of nurture and in doing so gave early twentieth-century differential psychology an unduly hereditarian bias.

The Early Mental Test Movement

The story of early mental testing has been so often and so well told that the present account can afford to be very brief.

Cattell returning to America from his doctoral studies with Wundt encountered Galton in Britain. Within a short period, he had tidied up and extended Galton's tests and specified their uses in psychology. He stated in his paper 'Mental tests' (1890) that a step towards giving psychology the certainty and exactness of the physical sciences 'could be made by applying a series of mental tests and measurements to a large number of individuals. The results would be of considerable scientific value in discovering the constancy of mental processes, their interdependence and their variation under different circumstances'. A little later Alfred Binet (1857–1911), in a paper with Henri entitled 'La psychologie individuelle', rounded out these objectives by adding (i) the study of the extent and nature of variations of the psychic processes from one individual to another and (ii) the determination of the interrelations of these various processes in any single individual as to whether they are mutually dependent or whether some are fundamental processes upon which all others depend.

Cattell's main list of tests comprised hand dynamometer pressure, rate of movement, two point tactile discrimination, pain sensitivity, weight discrimination, reaction time for sound, time for naming colours, bisection of a 50 centimetre line, judgement of a 10 seconds interval, and immediate memory span for random sets of letters. In addition he listed fifty other tests of a similar type. He pointed out the need for standardized methods of administration and of scoring if comparisons were to be made either between individuals or between groups and stressed the need for data derived from application of the tests to large groups in order to establish what later came to be called norms. He quickly set about the testing of large numbers of individuals, his principal pool of recruits being Columbia College students. Others prompted by him also began the application of mental tests, those in America usually having a practical objective in doing so. Binet in France also developed similar tests and applied them to a variety of individuals.

In 1901 Wissler working under Cattell delivered what seemed to be the *coup de grâce* to the high hopes of the early mental testers. Using Pearson's product–moment method of correlation he compared the scores of Columbia students on various mental tests, on various physical assessments and on academic grades. While the grades in various subjects correlated moderately with one another ($r = +0.30$ to $+0.75$), the scores on mental tests correlated negligibly, if at all, with one another ($r = -0.09$ to $+0.19$) and with academic grades. Even gymnasium grades correlated ($r = +0.53$) with average academics grades! Binet seems to have obtained similarly disappointing results in other situations though he did not have the correlation method to specify the degree of independence amongst his several tests.

Two strokes of genius rescued mental tests from their unpromising beginning. The first was a set of theoretical insights achieved by Charles Spearman (1863–1945) in Britain and the second a practical insight achieved by Binet.

Spearman's Contributions

Spearman in 1904 published two papers which contained the germinal ideas, the development of which occupied the greater part of his very productive life's work.

His first paper demonstrated that low correlations could result from contamination of test scores by a large error component and from the use of samples of unduly restricted range. He also argued that confusion would be produced by the use of very small samples as a consequence of sampling variation. He produced formulae whereby correlation coefficients could be corrected for attenuation by error and for reduction by a restricted range of the sample. The former correction was achieved by means of a reliability coefficient (estimated from the re-administration of a test) and the latter by means of dispersion estimates derived from unrestricted samples. Psychometric theory as unfolded by Spearman and others in the following fifty years sprang largely from these basic insights.

His second paper argued that, by using pairs of similar tests (in place of re-administrations of a single test) in what was essentially the correction for attenuation formula, it could be shown that the correlations, whatever their degrees, between tests of intellective functions could be accounted for by reference to a single general factor. This factor was deemed to enter into, or to saturate, different tests to different degrees. Further each test in addition to its *g* factor and its error component was said by him to have its specific or *s* factor. Later he produced more refined methods of making this analysis, through test intercorrelations, of the factor saturations of tests. Though some may dispute it, he may be properly claimed as the originator of the technique of factor analysis.

Spearman's two-factor, i.e. $g + s$, theory was vigorously opposed on several scores. First, there were those, for example Thorndike in America and Thomson in Britain, who argued that the communality between test scores which Spearman attributed to the *g* factor could be accounted for in other ways. The American spirit was generally loath to accept what seemed to be tinkering with data. Correction for attenuation seemed a bit too much like painting out Cromwell's warts. It must be admitted that Spearman's earlier analyses came out a little too pat, and that the research tactics of some of his supporters did savour too much of tinkering. Thomson's objection was at once both more technical and more philosophical. It would not be appropriate to go into it here beyond saying that he was right in claiming that the indirect verification of a hypothesis does not prove it and that alternative hypotheses verified by the same data should not be ignored. At the same time it is my view that Spearman's was inherently a more promising hypothesis than Thomson's. A second objection was directed to the weight Spearman made his *g* factor bear. Only reluctantly he came to admit 'broad' specific factors. At an early stage Burt (b. 1883) argued that the evidence indicated group factors (that is, factors covering a broad range of tests such as a verbal factor and a numerical factor) additional to the *g* factor. Kelley and later Thurstone pressed the argument further urging that group factors could without support from a general factor account for the observed patterns of test intercorrelations. However, when still later Thurstone began to speak of correlated first-order group factors and a second-order general factor he withdrew from this extreme view.

Little of the series of intricate technical argument and

counter-argument summarized above would have been possible had mental tests and statistical methods remained as they were at the beginning of the century.

Binet's Contribution

Part of the trouble with early mental tests as exposed by Wissler lay in large errors of measurement and constricted range of talent in the samples used but a major part lay in the very 'narrow' forms of mental functioning which they tested – in Spearman's terms, the s-factor saturations were too high and the g-factor saturations too low. A few early test devisers, Ebbinghaus with his completion test being one of them, had not fallen into this elementarist trap, but their avoidance of it was not remarked upon at the time. Under the pressure of a practical demand, Binet showed clearly how it was to be avoided. His task was to provide a means of recognizing and classifying children of deficient intelligence for admission to special institutions. He rejected as inadequate for the purpose ordinary medical and paedagogical examinations on the ground that they were assessments of other things. He urged instead a psychological examination which consisted of a graded series of short heterogeneous tasks requiring comprehension, judgement, reasoning and invention. It was not any *a priori* consideration which led him to this view but his extensive experience with the early tests of simple functions and his studies of the growth and exercise of the so-called higher mental functions in children. By insisting on heterogeneity in the tasks he was able to counterbalance the various s-factors entering the tests and by stressing comprehension, judgement, reasoning and invention he was able to find tasks with high g-saturations. He did not think of what he was doing in these Spearmanian terms but, granted that theory, that is what he did. With Simon, he produced, as is well known, his series of tests first in 1905 and then in revised form in 1908. Several empirical criteria had to be met by tests included in the scale. The tests had to show a decreasing average difficulty with increasing age in the children, they had to have a substantial degree of inter-test consistency, and they had as a whole to give results conforming with assessments of the children's intelligence made by teachers who knew the children and who were deemed to understand the difference between scholastic attainment and potential intelligence. The 1908 scale introduced a grouping together of tests in age blocks, and on the basis of this the assessment of intelligence was made in terms of mental age.

The scale was an immediate practical success. Binet revised it himself once more (1911), and translations and revisions were produced in other countries. The most notable English language version was the Stanford Revision of the Binet Scale produced by Lewis Terman in 1916. It was this version which adopted Stern's earlier proposed intelligence quotient.

Later Developments

Because we are reaching the point where the story of differential psychology to be given here may be brought to an end, just six later developments will be sketched. The first consisted of the production of other tests of intelligence to supplement the Binet Scale or to substitute for it in special circumstances. Quite early were performance tests, for example those of William Healy and Grace Fernald (1911) to supplement the predominantly verbal medium of the Binet; soon after group tests were developed both in the verbal and in non-verbal media. Later came special aptitude tests devised usually for educational or vocational uses. Most lacked the specificity of the early tests and were extremely valuable to the factor analysts who set out to discover the structure of human intellectual powers.

The second consisted of the much less successful attempts to assess quantitatively the orectic functions. Nevertheless the wide array of questionnaires, rating scales, behaviour tests and projective techniques have shed some light, dim and flickering though it be, on this side of human nature.

The third consisted of the attempts to study growth, the shape of the growth curve, the age at which it reaches its maximum and the like. Related to this was the fourth, namely the attempt to unravel the determinants of individual differences. Nature versus nurture has received special attention. Intellective tests being better than orectic assessments, more progress has been made in both these sets of endeavours when addressed to intelligence. Again related to the fourth has been the study of group differences – between the sexes, between social classes and between races. In all three endeavours, workers have tended to run beyond their resources, the techniques of assessment available to them, the understanding of the relations between the various functions and the techniques of disentangling the effects of various conditions.

The sixth development, the attempt to uncover the structure of human intellect and human temperament has been carried out largely by the application of factor analysis to the scores of individuals on a number of diverse tests. The main outlines of human intellect, that is, the main groups of interdependent functions, are now reasonably clear though there naturally enough remain disputes about matters of detail and about modes of expressing the better established results. The situation in respect of temperament, interests and attitudes is less clear but it is far from totally obscure. With the clarification of these structures improvements in the tests have been made possible and in turn better opportunities provided for the establishment of the patterns of growth, for the specification of sex differences and for the separation of the contributions of nature and nurture to individual differences.

Though a great deal of the work in the now flourishing differential psychology has been carried out in relative independence of general psychology, a number of important technical, theoretical and practical links have been forged. For instance, technical links have been formed between psychophysics (at the very core of traditional experimental psychology) and the psychometric theory developed from Spearman onwards. Again, it is recognized by many that differential psychology has much to say about the set of conditions symbolized by O in Woodworth's formula S–O–R. Finally in the attempt to make psychology useful to man differential psychology has proved perhaps the most valuable branch of the subject. For that it now is, a branch grafted on to the main tree and no longer a separate plant; it is a branch, however, which bears quite distinctive fruit.

8 The Assimilation of Medical Psychology

Medical psychology which grew together with general psychology both in its philosophical and scientific phases more often than differential psychology did has proved more difficult to graft. Perhaps there is some degree of mutual auto-immunity. Indeed at times what looks like a graft is no more than an intertwined branch of another plant with its own roots. Perhaps symbiosis may be a better image than graft. At least one can say that general psychology and medical psychology now grow closely together, mutually nourishing each other and in the course of doing so mutually assimilating to each other. There appear to be several reasons for this state of affairs. General experimental psychology and its philosophical and physiological antecedents have as we have seen been strongly cognitive. Even where attention has been given to feelings they have been given a cognitive twist, markedly in the psychology of content but also to a degree in act psychology and in early functionalism. The presupposition that mind is consciousness had a prevailing cognitive emphasis. On the other hand medical psychology even when concerned with cognitive disorders such as hallucinations and delusions could hardly avoid the impression that it was dealing with inlying forces, and dark forces at that. Again the framework within which general psychology worked was one of rationality, whereas medical psychology had to cope with the irrational, with an array of phenomena where commonsense could hardly be a guide. Finally, mysticism has been a common companion of medical psychology. It is almost as though the two psychologies were in incompatible sap groups.

Demonic Possession

Mental derangement and related pathological phenomena have long been recognized, described and variously explained. It will be sufficient for the present purpose to begin with the medieval and early modern explanation in terms of demonic possession. The irrationality of insanity, its apparent contrariety to nature's (if not God's) orderliness and the transparent evil of much of it, whether to the person himself or to his associates, seemed to betoken only one possible origin. The obvious method of treatment was exorcism which often succeeded through suggestion if for no other reason. In the late Middle Ages the notion of derangement through possession became mixed with that of witchcraft, an association that remained firm into at least the seventeenth century. The infamous *Malleus Malificarum* (1684), the work of two Dominicans, contains in addition to advice on the detection, conviction and punishment of witches a good deal of information about deviant behaviour, most of it overtly sexual. This last is not surprising as Kraemer and Sprenger held that a devil possessed a witch ordinarily through copulation with her. As the ultimate salvation of the immortal soul was more important than the comforts of the possessed body, physical punishments to the extremes of drowning and burning in order to make the body an intolerable refuge for the devil were added to the spiritual rites of exorcism. Even though the belief in possession had disappeared the eighteenth-century cure for insanity by frequent prolonged cold baths in icy climates and the twentieth-century electro-convulsive therapy are worthy if milder successors to the prescriptions of the *Malleus*.

The Recognition of Mental Disorder as Illness

With the waning of a belief in possession, a belief in the insane as evil, perverse and degenerate remained; their incarceration under inhumane conditions was as much to punish them as to keep them out of harm's way and to prevent them from harming, annoying and distressing others. But by the late eighteenth century more advanced thinkers were arguing that the insane were ill not evil. In 1793 Pinel removed the chains from many of the inmates of the Asylum de Bicêtre and when later he took charge of La Salpêtrière he established a regime of study and medical care in replacement of the inordinate bloodletting, purging and ducking that had previously been the lot of its deranged women patients. This humane attitude, often under a kindlier religious motivation than moved the authors of the *Malleus*, began to manifest itself elsewhere. But more important in the long run was the earnest endeavour to study the insane. Esquirol in France following the lead given by Pinel attempted a classification of mental disorder. A line of successors in France and later in Germany culminated in Emil Kraepelin (1855–1927), a former student of Wundt's. He brought his training in experimental psychology to bear on the ill-defined problems which confronted him. In addition to studies on sleep, on fatigue and on the effect of various drugs on mental processes, he produced a systematic classification of mental disease which forms the basis of its modern taxonomy. He put his classification forward tentatively, admitting the uncertainty of much of his knowledge and of his conceptions of aetiology. It is worthy of summary:

(1) Disorders of infection, e.g. fever delirium
(2) Disorders of exhaustion, e.g. collapse delirium and acquired neurasthenia
(3) Intoxication disorders, e.g. alcoholic paranoia, morphinism
(4) Thyroigenous psychoses, e.g. myxoedematous insanity and cretinism
(5) Dementia praecox (i) hebephrenia, (ii) catatonic and (iii) paranoid
(6) Dementia paralytica
(7) Organic dementias, e.g. Huntington's chorea, multiple sclerosis, cerebral tumour and cerebral apoplexy

(8) Involutional psychoses, e.g. melancholia and senile dementia

(9) Manic-depressive insanity, including manic, depressive and mixed states

(10) Paranoia

(11) Epileptic psychoses

(12) Psychogenic neuroses, e.g. hysteria and traumatic neurosis

(13) Constitutional psychopathic states, e.g. despondency, compulsive insanity and contrary sexual instincts

(14) Psychopathic personalities, e.g. moral insanity, morbid liars and the unstable

(15) Defective mental development, e.g. imbecility and idiocy

It is clear that this is not simply a grouping by symptoms. It is also a grouping by causes. Judgements about the latter were often wrong, but until some methodical grouping had been made the search for causes could only be confused and biased, and the search for cures based primarily on rule-of-thumb and pure hunch. An interesting point for our story is this growing together in Kraepelin's work of the two psychological traditions – experimental and medical.

A Significant Side Issue

In the late eighteenth century, Mesmer picking up an idea supported by Paracelsus and later van Helmont assumed an influence exercised by magnets on the human body. This doctrine had been associated with the mysterious force from the stars alleged to influence man's destiny. Beginning with magnets, but later abandoning them, Mesmer induced a number of phenomena which he attributed to animal magnetism emanating from the mesmerist. Prominent among these were what we now recognize as suggestion and hypnotism. He surrounded his demonstrations with mystical trappings and evoked as much scepticism as acceptance amongst his medical confreres. Others in the nineteenth century took up mesmerism as an aid to medicine. Prominent amongst them were Elliotson, a founder of the University College Hospital, London (his support for mesmerism finally cost him his association with University College and its hospital) and Esdaile, who in Ceylon demonstrated its anaesthetic value in surgery. It was James Braid who really brought these phenomena to earth (circa 1845), likening the trance state to sleep and giving it a name which finally became hypnosis (Greek *hypnos*, sleep). He insisted that not only had magnets nothing to do with the phenomena but also that there was no animal magnetism or other force emanating from a potent mesmerist. He attributed the phenomena instead to processes in the person, expectations arising from suggestion coupled with a narrowing of attention. He had found that having the subject stare at an object was particularly effective in inducing the hypnotic state and argued that the immobility of the eye muscles was a relevant circumstance in the narrowing of attention.

Interest in hypnosis passed mainly to France which was able to provide a more congenial atmosphere for it. Liébeault, a physician in Nancy, led the way in the 1860s and later recruited Bernheim, another physician there, to the use of hypnosis in medical practice. An active school also developed in Paris under the leadership of Jean Charcot (1825–93), who established a notable neurological clinic at La Salpêtrière. His work interested and influenced Ribot who, though not an experimentalist, was given charge in 1885 of a course in experimental and comparative psychology at the Sorbonne, and who four years later was appointed to a chair and established a psychological laboratory under Beaunis and Binet.

Liébeault and Bernheim stressed the psychological aspects of hypnosis, arguing that suggestion played a crucial role in it. They used hypnotherapy for a number of general medical complaints, recognizing what is now referred to as the psychosomatic component in illness. Charcot, working mainly with hysterical patients at La Salpêt-rière, adopted a contrary view. He believed that hypnotiz-ability was a distinctive feature of hysterics and of persons predisposed to hysteria (hysteroid personalities as they came to be called). He attributed hysteria to a physiologi-cal state of degeneracy. Though he was wrong in these views, he deserves great credit for his thorough, if often misguided, investigation of hysteria. He paid particular attention to sensory and motor symptoms – anaesthesias of the most bizarre sort, hyperaesthesia, paralyses and epi-leptoid convulsions. Oddly some of the symptoms he reported were the product of his methods of examination, the spiral field of vision being a notable example. Despite the physiological emphasis he noted many other symptoms of a more clearly psychological sort such as amnesia, exci-tability and dissociated states. Not unimportant was his view of the phases through which hypnosis passed, namely, lethargy, catalepsy and somnambulism. In the third and deepest phase of hypnosis he recognized that activities went on of which the patient was unaware, that a splitting of the psychic economy occurred. Others had propounded the idea of unconscious activity, for example Carpenter's notion of unconscious cerebration, and this was a seemingly empirical reinforcement of it.

Though others were busily working on the more ex-treme forms of mental disorder and thereby contributing to the development of psychiatry, this concentration of Charcot on neurosis was especially significant for medical psychology as it is being considered here. The neurotic is in so many ways less far removed from the normal than the psychotic that a psychology of neurosis has a greater opportunity of forming links with the psychology of the normal. Indeed the division between the neurotic and the normal is so blurred that the two psychologies should be able to merge – only their traditions and their presupposi-tions can prevent this.

The Emergence of Dynamic Depth Psychology

In the closing years of the nineteenth century several medical psychologists were developing psychogenic theories of the neuroses or psychoneuroses as they preferred to call them. Outstanding amongst them were Pierre Janet (1859–1949) in France and Sigmund Freud (1856–1939) in Austria, the former a protégé of Charcot and the latter one of his visiting pupils. There were many others, most of whom began as enthusiastic users of hypnosis as a method of investigation and treatment.

Janet and Freud, like Charcot, concentrated on the neuroses, but unlike him stressed the role of mental forces conceived in affective and conative terms in the causation of these disorders. In doing this they provided a complement to the overwhelming emphasis on cognition which was characteristic of general psychology. They also stressed initially in their interpretations emotionally traumatic experiences which though lost to consciously accessible memory were nevertheless still effective. It is in respect of these two features, energies and non-conscious functioning, that they may properly be called dynamic depth psychologists. There was, however, a basic difference in their views of the way mental energies worked in the production of neurosis. Briefly put, Janet's view was that the neurotic lacked sufficient mental energy to hold his psyche together in a state of integration; as a result parts of it functioned in disassociation from the rest. Freud's view by contrast, was that there were diverse mental energies which were in conflict with one another. Dominant forces repressed those at variance with them and in the neurotic this repression was so ineffectively achieved as to render the mental situation unmanageable and intolerable. Janet never unfolded his views in any extensive way wheras Freud, a man of much greater originality, has often been thought to have let his theories run away with him – he certainly went well beyond his facts.

Both Janet and Freud had some acquaintance with the

new general psychology. Freud, though trained as a neurologist, took some courses given by Brentano and at the latter's suggestion translated the collected works of John Stuart Mill into German. He was not, however, completely empiricist in temper. Though a sensitive observer, his views were tinged with rationalism and he was given to intuitionism. Janet might have succeeded in grafting medical psychology on to general psychology. He was sufficiently within the latter tradition to succeed Ribot at the Sorbonne. However it was his fate to be overshadowed by a more original and independent mind. Though he had his followers and though he produced a number of able students, including Jean Piaget, Janet is now largely forgotten, whereas Freud is still so towering a figure that others feel that they must be either for him or against him. Indeed his views were so complex, were so subject to subtle change and covered so wide a range of topics that one wonders whether anything illuminating can be said in exposition and comment in a few pages. Nevertheless the attempt must be made.

Psychoanalysis

Psychoanalysis as founded and developed by Freud is at once a method of observation, a therapy and a theory. A central tenet of the theory asserts unconscious or, as Freud's word *unbewusst* would have been better translated, unbeknown mental functioning. Quite early Freud emphasized that hysterical symptoms were the symbolic expression of 'memories', not accessible to the conscious person or self, of earlier traumatic experiences. These emotionally charged memories were unconscious not by mere default, not through the lack of sufficient integrating energy, but through a positive process of exclusion from consciousness. Such repression was the consequence of conflict between incompatible forces. Later Freud argued that a traumatic experience was not required to produce a conflict of such intensity that it could be resolved only by the repression of one of the warring forces. Indeed he argued that conflict was inherent in mental life and repression part of the whole process of mental development. Both mental health and mental illness were conditioned by repression, the former by successful repression and the latter by unsuccessful repression.

Throughout the long unfolding of the theory – it was changed as well as elaborated – Freud tended to assume two sets of opposing psychic forces or instincts. Early he spoke of the sex instincts versus the moral instincts. Later of libido versus ego, and finally of eros (the life or creative energies) versus thanatos (the death instinct). At first he held that it was the sexual energies (or libido) which suffered repression, and probably on that account concentrated on the clarification of them. The moral instincts (or ego instincts) being in consciousness could be taken more or less for granted. Sexual desire or libido was conceived much more widely than the sex instinct had traditionally been. It was deemed to be a fund of energy subject to differentiation. It had an aim (basically sensual gratification), objects to which it became attached and organs through which it was gratified or expressed. Its source was excitation somewhere in the body and its aim could also be thought of as the release of this excitation. Certain regions of the body, spoken of as erogenous zones, were particularly invested with libido; special stress was placed on the oral, anal and genital zones. These form part of the basis of distinction between the component sexual instincts, such as the oral, anal and genital instincts which seek their gratification through those organs. In addition, there are component instincts connected with seeing or being seen (scoptophilic and exhibitionistic), and with the infliction or the suffering of pain (sadistic and masochistic). That they were all of a kind, however, was deemed to be evidenced by the way they reinforced one another and were transformed one into another. Important use of this contention was made in the explanation of sexual perversions.

A third important part of the theory dealt with psychosexual development. Libido was deemed to be operative in the infant, predominantly in undifferentiated form, then unfolding in later infancy and young childhood through oral, anal and genital phases. The mother was deemed to be an early object of libidinal attachment, thus creating an Oedipus situation ultimately leading to the repression of aggression directed to the father and genital desire toward the mother, thus forming the Oedipus complex and leading to a sexually latent period from which the person emerges in early adolescence. Two important factors in mental disorder were deemed to be fixation or a failure to grow adequately into the next phase and regression or a return to an earlier phase. In infancy mental life is lived in accordance with the pleasure principle, an attempt to gain maximum gratification for minimum effort in disregard of reality. In general the unconscious forces continue to operate in this way, though the principle is also to be seen in conscious processes, for example fantasy. Gradually, however, the reality principle is increasingly adopted at the conscious level and the ego emerges.

Later Freud came to assert three major structures in the psychic economy. The Id, or non-person, is largely unconscious and the residence of the greater part of libido; the Ego is largely conscious or accessible to consciousness, and being dominated by the reality principle is the part of the mind in closest contact with external reality and its possibilities and demands; and the Super-ego, akin to moral conscience, which because of the harshness of some of its demands is also largely unconscious. The Super-ego is based on the introjected image of the mother and incorporates the demands of the parents on the child; it takes the place of the parents in the management of Id impulses.

Finally mention must be made of the mental mechanisms that serve at once to defend the Ego and to enable the gratification of repressed impulses. Indeed repression may be thought of as the principal mechanism: it excludes from consciousness what would be intolerable to the Ego but it does not annihilate the unwanted impulses for they still flourish even if in inhibited and distorted ways. Others are displacement, symbolization, reaction formation, projection, conversion, identification, sublimation and rationalization, most of which have been adopted as part of the stock-in-trade of the general psychology of personality, normal and abnormal.

Though it began as a contribution to psychopathology, psychoanalytic theory quickly expanded into a more general theory. The interpretation of dreams, the explanation of slips of the tongue and of the pen, and an account of the psychic origins of art, religion and society were added by Freud. Splinter groups developed within the psychoanalytic movement and indeed are still developing. A central orthodox group, however, has always remained faithful to Freud. Though met continually with resistance, the whole movement, but Freud in particular, has had an extensive and profound influence. Literature and literary criticism, art, morality and even religion have felt this influence. General psychology has also been greatly influenced, indeed it has assimilated a great deal of psychoanalytic theory. Nevertheless it is difficult to argue that it has incorporated it. The analysts have an explanation of this. What Freud is said to have uncovered is said to be in all of us and we are loath to admit it; only if each of us were psychoanalysed could we do so. Now it is true of any science that its practitioners cannot unaided manipulate its technical and conceptual tools. But something more than that is being demanded here. Not having had the benefit of analysis, I see other explanations. First, the distinction between fact and theory is even more blurred than elsewhere in science. Every alleged fact produced by the psychoanalytic method is already interpreted within the theoretical framework. Second, the theory in its explanatory role is too facile. Many of the concepts are so slippery as to defy precise empirical application and the implications of the major propositions are so diverse as to cover almost any eventuality. Thus though in one sense empirically verifiable, the theories are not empirically falsifiable. There has been much argument pro and con on this point. Indeed it has even been asked whether psychoanalytic findings are verifiable – a question prompted no doubt by the extent to which theory suffuses what are said to be the facts of observation. Third, psychoanalysis has not shaken off the strong mystical attachments which have bedevilled the whole history of medical psychology. Mysticism was strongest in Jung's analytical psychology but it was also present in orthodox psychoanalytic theory.

9 Two Revolutions Within

Before the contemporary scene can be set, two revolutions within the traditions of general experimental psychology must be sketched. One, originating in the interaction between the two great European movements, produced Gestalt theory or more generally holistic cognitive theory. The other occurred within American functionalism and produced behaviourism or S–R theory. They both began in the second decade of this century, a time at which the invasion from medical psychology was entering an active phase. It seems desirable to preface the broad account of each with some remarks on the premonitions of what was to come.

Holism and Phenomenology

As already reported act psychology became increasingly interested in whole qualities and adopted increasingly a phenomenological viewpoint. Nor was the psychology of content uninfluenced by these tendencies. Krueger, who was Wundt's student and from 1917 his successor at Leipzig, formulated a *Ganzheitspsychologie* in which primacy was given to *Komplexqualitäten* in experience. Interestingly Krueger admitted a debt to both Wundt and Cornelius. Mention has already been made of the work in G. E. Müller's laboratory which had a strong phenomenological flavour. Schumann who had been a collaborator with Müller carried out after his move to Stumpf's laboratory at Berlin a most extensive series of experimental investigations of visual spatial patterning which he reported at length between 1900 and 1904.

Both movements experienced disagreements within themselves as well as between themselves on how whole qualities were to be regarded and explained, and in this there was much crossing of the floor to vote with what was otherwise the opposition. Wundt tended to regard whole qualities as emergents from the fusion and other compounding of elements, von Ehrenfels as another type of basic content, Meinong as additional contents founded by special superordinate acts working on the foundational contents, Cornelius as founded attributes inherent in the experience of wholes and Schumann as products of attention which took together the components it selected from potential experience. Perhaps there were some, though they are hard to find, who took whole qualities as mere summations of elements.

Holism was also expressing itself in other ways. For instance Stern in the early years of the century was formulating a personalisitic developmental psychology which was both purposivist and holist. But this was not peculiarly continental. James, as we have seen, had holistic tendencies and Stout was even more markedly holistic in his thinking.

Gestalt Theory

It is conceivable that Gestalt theory as formulated by Wertheimer (1880–1943), Koffka (1886–1941) and Köhler (1887–1967) could have evolved painlessly from these earlier lines of thought; indeed there were some who maintained that it had nothing new in it. However, it seemed to its proponents that radical reforms were required and that only a revolution could re-establish psychology on a sound basis. There was something new in it but to make clear what that was the revolutionaries caricatured rather than characterized what they were revolting against.

The first shot was fired in 1912 by Wertheimer in his report on his studies of apparent movement. The shot was not as devastating as the Gestalt theorists later made it out to be, but no doubt, like the fall of the Bastille, it was symbolic. However rather than tell once again the story in its chronological order, it will be more profitable here to state the proposed new constitution for psychology.

Foremost amongst the articles is a phenomenological set. The determinants of mental processes, or behaviour as the Gestalt theorists came to say after their migration to America, are to be sought in the phenomenal world. This is not the world as it is in itself, the 'real' or physical world, but the world, including the person himself, as it appears to him to be. The phenomenal world consists of objects in relation with one another, it is not made up of compounds or complexes of elementary components. Anyone, it is said, taking the phenomenal world as it comes, that is, not seeing it through some special analytic screen, cannot be unaware of this. This article has often been mistaken as anti-analytic. However the Gestalt theorists were not opposed to the structural analysis of experience. What they rejected was the abstractive analysis into elements which were not in experience to begin with and which had to be 'synthesized' in order that one could get back to the experience one began with. In chemistry, elements may be found, in experiment if not always in nature, in a free state; in psychology, it has been widely admitted, elementary sensations, images, feelings, forms and thoughts are never observed, they are abstractions. Thus the Gestalt theorists reject (i) the distinction between sensation and perception and (ii) attention which was alleged to pick out and group particular components from amongst the myriad deemed to be potentially present at any moment. A related article asserts that experience is had immediately and primarily as a structured totality. Part properties do not determine whole properties but are determined by them. *Gestalt* is said to be one of the categories, or fundamental states of being, indeed one superordinate to many of those traditionally listed.

Another basic set of articles asserts that the phenomenal world is a dynamic field in the sense in which fields of forces are spoken of in modern physics. It is these interacting forces which organize the field. Sometimes the phenomenal field is in a state of equilibrium and so there is a stable, constant phenomenal world. But in various circumstances, the equilibrium is disturbed and the field is restructured. Reversible figures provide a simple perceptual example. The laws of perceptual grouping indicate some of the factors involved in this play of forces. The primacy asserted of *Gestalten* in perception and such notions as good figure, i.e. states of equilibrium, have often been mistaken as a resurgence of nativism. It is true that a denial of the empiristic view is involved. The empiristic and the nativistic views are contraries not contradictories, hence a denial of the former does not entail an affirmation of the latter. It was not alleged that the structure of experience is innate. It is the product of the interplay of forces in the field. The concept of force, always rather elusive in its connotation, is especially vague in Gestalt theory. Lewin (1890–1947) in his version of the theory did a little to clarify it by saying that it was a vector, a directed force relating a state of tension in the person and an object with demand characteristics. But even this is largely a promissory note. The notion of gravitational force would be of little explanatory value without a formula like Newton's and relatively independent estimates of masses and distances. Explanations in terms of forces which were offered by Gestalt theory usually have a *post hoc* quality.

A third set of articles relates to isomorphism. Through them bridges between the phenomenal field, brain fields and stimulus fields were provided. A central problem for any phenomenalism, whether that of Locke, that of Johannes Müller or that of phenomenology, is finding a way for saying anything about the 'real' world. Locke tried to provide it through the primary qualities and Müller through a somewhat similar device. Köhler, however, argued not for some kind of mirror image in the phenomenal world of features in the 'real' world. Instead he argued for isomorphism mediated by the nervous system. It may be doubted that this bridge is any more able to carry the traffic.

The Gestalt theorists were as active in experimental research as they were in theorizing and in controversy. The greater part of their early work was on perception, mainly visual. It made many new descriptive contributions. Many of the phenomena described revealed inadequacies in earlier theories. This should not be surprising, for the Gestalt theorists in their experimentation were looking for crucial data pointing away from the interpretations their opponents favoured. Thus in his 1912 report Wertheimer used the occurrence of the pure *phi* phenomenon, that is seen movement without the seeing of what moves, to show that apparent movement elicited by successive displaced stimuli cannot be the result of any kind of compounding of the part experiences (the separately located components). Likewise later work, showing that familiar 'figures' were not seen when embedded in larger novel figures produced by factors such as continuity, symmetry and *prägnanz*, was used as evidence against the empiristic explanation of the structure of the perceptual field. The laws of perceptual grouping, the role of contour, the remarkable phenomenon of light black demonstrated by Gelb, and field factors involved in the phenomenal constancies are among the empirical contributions.

Other cognitive processes were investigated in the same theoretical vein. These included decay in memory and creative thinking. Both were treated as a restructuring of the cognitive field through the interplay of field forces. Quite early in the piece Köhler's work on problem solving by chimpanzees led him to argue against Thorndike's view of animal learning as an uncomprehending blundering by trial and error through an incomprehensible world. The suddenness of solutions led him to argue that the animal attained insight through the restructuring of the cognitive field. In this case, of course, the subject could not describe his field; the experimenter had to infer it or more precisely guess about it from the animal's behaviour. In their studies of creative thinking and of problem solving, the Gestalt theorists struck a blow for intelligence as something other than innate ideas or acquired associations or correct responses to the fragmentary tasks of intelligence tests.

Though not alone in doing so, Lewin, who stood a little outside the central movement, must be given the main credit for work in the field of action, motivation and personality dynamics. Though his terminology was often different his concepts overlapped those of Gestalt theory. Once again, his theorizing was illustrated and defended by an array of observations which were both ingenuously made and valuable in that they provided a challenge for alternative theories.

As time went on other psychologists in the wider *Ganzheit* movement made common cause with the Gestalt theorists in opposition to elementarism, reductionism and antiphenomenalism as manifested in behaviourism.

Objectivism, Mechanism and Realism

A variety of methodological, metaphysical and epistemological lines of thought provide the background for the behaviourist revolution. Three of them will be stressed here.

The first is methodological. In the early phases of modern psychology introspection was taken to be the royal road to psychological data. There were of course niceties of distinction between the refined introspections of trained observers adopting an analytic attitude and the more casual observations of untrained observers whether children replying to the oral questions of a Binet or adolescents responding to items in the questionnaire of a Stanley Hall. In addition, of course, were the interpretative observations by sophisticated Würzburg investigators of their own thinking and the interpretations by analysts of the free associations and dreams of psychologically unsophisticated subjects whether normal or neurotic. In contrast to these many varieties of subjective data, there were from the very beginning objective data for psychology to consider. The difference between 'I see a yellow square' and 'His reaction time is 0.3 seconds' is that only the observer himself can vouch for the former datum whereas any number of bystanders may corroborate the latter. There can be, of course, a sort of corroboration by consensus in the former case. Several observers may be asked to fixate a given blue square for a minute and then to look at a neutral grey projection field. All of them may say 'I see a yellow square', but each is reporting his own after-image, and there is always justification for a nagging doubt that one observer's yellow may be another's green or still another's orange. An idealist or strict phenomenalist may have similar doubts about objective data but the working scientist, whatever his epistemology may be, acts as though he were a realist when dealing with external events. The early psychologist usually treated his objective data as indicative of subjective events not accessible to him. In his study of animals, of young children and of some types of deranged person, he had no access through the subject's report to psychic events, but he could interpret the overt behaviour available for his observation in terms of inner events. Increasingly, however, many psychologists came to value objective data in their own right. For instance in 1904 James Cattell argued in these terms. It was only a short step from that position to the more radical one which maintains that objective data about behaviour constitute a firmer basis for a science than do the subjective data about inner psychic events. The more radical view is methodological behaviourism.

The second important line of thought is mechanism, which was closely associated with nineteenth-century materialism and which opposed vitalism in biology. The latter doctrine held that, although there are physico-chemical processes in the living organism, some living principle is there as well. Drawing on very old ideas, the vitalists argued that there are successive levels in nature, the higher subsuming but adding to the lower. The added features were held not to be deducible from or reducible without remainder to the features characteristic of the lower. Thus it was commonly said that there is matter, life and mind, each on its own level. Sometimes society was named as a fourth level. The materialists often in a simple-minded way denied this view, maintaining that an adequate knowledge of matter would provide the key to unlock the mysteries of the whole universe. The vitalists and mentalists maintained that such manifest features of living organisms as adaptation, self-maintenance and reproduction, such manifest features of animals as purposiveness, sensitivity and variable responsiveness and such manifest features of man as cognition, including reason and will, were inexplicable in materialistic terms. The mechanists argued in retort that these features would either dissolve with the advance of science or would be seen to be complex cases of the mechanistic laws which in the physical realm had replaced earlier animistic and teleological thinking. This was part of the background of what has been called metaphysical behaviourism, that is the denial of a special mental subject matter for psychology and not merely the denial that such topics were amenable to scientific study.

There is another source of metaphysical behaviourism which has been often overlooked, namely the epistemological doctrine of realism. It may be best understood in contrast with subjective idealism and phenomenalism which were potent influences on early scientific psychology. The common man is said to be a naïve realist in that he believes that with a few exceptions the world is really as he perceives it. There are, independently of his knowing them, stones as he sees them, noises as he hears them and people as he experiences them. If he is a little critical he acknowledges that he sometimes mistakes the world – he has illusions and possibly even hallucinations (he usually doubts that his dreams are veridical) – and that some things escape his knowledge (perhaps he admits that they do so only in fact and not through some inherent quality of inaccessibility). Ranged against him are a formidable array of philosophers variously known as phenomenalists and idealists. They include Locke, Berkeley and many others. Though varying in their formulations, they hold that we do not have any direct knowledge of external objects, and that what we know is constituted by its being known. In extreme form they question the right of any one to speak informatively about external objects. All we know directly are impressions, sensations, ideas or more generally mental states. As many of these states seem to have an external reference, some phenomenalists are prepared to accept that there are things beyond our ideas. Thus they are ready to argue that ideas and impressions provide an indirect knowledge of the external world or that they provide a basis for us to construct theories about that world. As we have seen, Wundt maintained that psychology was the study of our immediate direct experience and almost every nineteenth-century psychologist held some analogous view. Realists maintain that directly knowable objects exist independently of their being known. An American group of New Realists were vigorously propounding this view at the end of the first decade of this century. Perry and Holt (1912) in particular denied that knowns were other than independently existing objects and situations. Knowing in their view was not the generation in the knower of sensations, ideas or more generally phenomena; it was a discriminative response made by the organism to objects and situations. Among the events to which a person might respond in this way were his other responses. In particular he might express this discrimination of his own responses verbally. This was their account of introspection. Consciousness as mental content thus vanished and introspection was assimilated to nonmental responses.

Radical Behaviourism

Behaviourism, like Gestalt theory, did not come out of a clear sky. There were many signs of it in the air before Watson (1878–1958) issued his manifesto in 1913. As has been mentioned, Cattell argued for objective observation as a psychological method in its own right; physiologists such as Loeb first in Germany but later in America, and Pavlov (1849–1936) in Russia had demonstrated how a great deal of animal behaviour could be studied and, it seemed, explained without resort to mentalistic concepts; finally some psychologists, e.g. McDougall and Pillsbury, had offered definitions of psychology in which behaviour was given as its subject of study. But again it seemed that a thunderbolt was needed to make it rain. Watson volunteered to play Zeus.

In his 1913 manifesto he placed greatest stress on the methodological argument. If psychology were to take its place amongst the natural sciences, it must abandon introspection and rely solely on objective observation. Only in this way, he argued, could the whims and prejudices of the observer be eliminated. He recognized that from this would follow a psychology without consciousness, without mentalistic concepts, but he seemed unready to attack these *per se* on metaphysical grounds. He went merely as far as saying if there is consciousness as described by the content psychologists and by the functionalists it is not amenable to scientific study and it is irrelevant for the explanation and prediction of objectively observed behaviour. Later other radical behaviourists were ready to make an unequivocal denial. For example Hunter (1889–1954) took up the realist's line and asserted that the objects of experience were part of the environment and in no way psychic.

However, Watson made it clear in 1913 that certain mentalist concepts were metaphysically objectionable. These included those assuming a mind-body dichotomy, as they perforce separated psychology from the other natural sciences. As he unfolded his psychology it became clearer that his was a metaphysical as well as a methodological behaviourism. In his 1919 textbook he states the task of psychology as the formulation 'through systematic observation and experimentation [of] the laws and principles which underlie man's reactions' in order that it may predict and control those reactions. Again, he says 'In each adjustment there is always both a *response* or *act* and a *stimulus* or *situation* which call[s] out that response' (pp. 9–10). The laws of psychology were to be stated in terms of stimuli and responses. To begin with almost as much stress was placed on hereditary as on acquired S–R connexions. Even instincts considered as innate tendencies to complex responses, but not as forces directed towards ends, had a place. They were seen as having, as habits do, adaptive functions but these were their consequences and not their causes. Teleology along with dualism was deemed to be unscientific. Later Watson, in common with the other radical behaviourists, moved to a more environmentalist position in which habit received an overwhelming stress. There had been in the period when behaviourism was being elaborated increasingly numerous and vigorous assaults on the instinct doctrine. These came from several sources – behaviourism itself, developmental functionalism and from sociology. More and more of what had been taken to be innate was found to be acquired. The behaviourists in their work as experimentalists were predominantly concerned with learning – maze-learning in animals, discrimination learning, the delayed response and the like. Watson's work on emotions in infancy revealed a much poorer innate endowment than his predecessors had assumed, and much of what had been taken to be intelligence and reasoning in both animals and children seemed reducible to complex habits. In the third decade of the century Pavlov's work became better known to English speaking psychologists. It was so much to the liking of the radical behaviorists that they incorporated most of it in their own system. Their psychology became more and more a psychology of learning, an associationism not of ideas but of stimuli and responses.

Perception had never been a topic of interest, though its rudiments in the form of sensory discrimination had some work done on them. Thought and language were fitted into the S–R framework; at first thinking received a motor interpretation, but later, together with language, its symbolic function was stressed. In radical behaviourism there was little place for motivation. Stimuli, both internal and external, served to initiate behaviour and to guide it; the only other energy involved was that provided by bodily processes to the effectors, the receptors and the connectors in the nervous system. Emotion was not, as James and Lange had said, the experience of certain kinds of visceral and muscular states, it was those states. Even Thorndike's law of effect formulated on the evidence of experiments on animals had to go. Satisfaction and annoyance were subjective states.

There were, of course, milder behaviourisms such as that of Tolman in which cognitive and purposive concepts objectively defined were retained. They were methodological rather than metaphysical behaviourisms and were consequently less radical departures from the functionalism from which behaviourism sprang. Later there were more sophisticated metaphysical behaviourisms such as that of Hull. It is beyond the task set here, however, to examine them.

Radical behaviourism provided a marked contrast with Gestalt theory. It was not only objective but it was anti-phenomenalist – the environment and the organism as they were in themselves provided the determinants of behaviour. It was elementarist and anti-emergentist. It rejected notions of mental forces and it was mechanist. Again though Gestalt theory was not radically nativist, it was in general not empiristic, whereas radical behaviourism came to stress the role of learning and habit. Finally whereas Gestalt theory by its very nature stressed perception and saw other processes in a cognitive light, radical behaviourism virtually banished perception and extracted from thinking, conceptualization, memory and learning their traditionally cognitive flavour.

Neither radical behaviourism nor Gestalt theory was effective in dealing with motivation. It is true, of course, that Tolman's purposive behaviourism and Hullian behaviourism did have a good deal to say on the matter just as Lewin's field theory did. Motivation and personality dynamics were promoted by some of the later functionalists and especially by the dynamic depth psychologists.

10 The Psychologies of 1925

The nineteen-twenties may be regarded as the period in which contemporary psychology was ushered in, although a stricter view of contemporary would name the nineteen-forties. The nineteen-twenties witnessed the propounding of an almost bewildering array of psychologies. They are often referred to as systems of psychology but that is an exaggerated term as most of them were not stated in systematic fashion and the few that have aspired to formal systematization are quite fragmentary compared with say mechanics, not to mention arithmetic, geometry and logic, where systems *par excellence* are to be found. 'Movements' may be a better term, reserving 'schools' for the particular sets of doctrines which may vary within a movement. Thus we speak of the dynamic depth psychology movement and within it the schools of Freud and the 'orthodox' psychoanalysts, of Jung and his fellow analytical psychologists, of Adler and his fellow individual psychologists, and of Janet, Prince and others stressing dissociation.

Murchison, in compiling his two collections, *Psychologies of 1925* and *Psychologies of 1930,* seems to have recognized ten or eleven 'isms' and his list is clearly not complete. His classifications are varied in width. Thus Janet's *L'Analyse psychologique,* Freudian psychoanalysis and Adlerian individual psychology share a single heading, whereas Hunter and Weiss share 'behaviourism', Woodworth and Dunlap each having his own label, 'dynamic psychology' and 'reaction psychology' respectively. Hunter, Weiss, Woodworth and Dunlap had as much in common as Janet, Freud (spoken for by Flugel) and Adler. But then McDougall had a separate heading and he might have appropriately been put amongst the analytical psychologists together with Jung, had the latter had a spokesman. A few of Murchison's 'isms' were in 1930 virtually if not actually defunct. Except in its new S–R form associationism was extinct, act psychology except amongst a few philosophers was dead (though it left a rich bequest to phenomenological psychology) and the elementarist psychology of content, if not down, was by 1930 'out' on its feet.

Woodworth writing in 1931 listed five schools, or six if one counts his own middle-of-the-road functionalism. Heidbreder in 1933 distinguished seven psychologies. From a more remote viewpoint I wish to distinguish four movements or types of psychology to be found in the nineteen-twenties when modern psychology passed into what is still contemporary psychology. They are S–R theory, cognitive theory, dynamic depth theory and typological or differential psychology. In the nineteen-twenties and since, they were all committed to the description, explanation and prediction of the conduct or behaviour of animals, especially men, in adjusting themselves to their environments and their environments to them. In this respect they were all functionalist to greater or less degree. They differed in where they considered the emphasis was to be put, in what the strategy and tactics were to be and in the stand they took on certain general issues, on certain attitudes to or views about nature and life.

Perhaps they may be the best first differentiated in terms of what they took to be the key to their task of describing, explaining and predicting behaviour. The S–R theorists considered this key to consist of the stimulus-response connexions or associations mediated by the nervous system, and so it set as its specific task the elucidation of the formation of these connexions, of the conditions which activated them and of the ways in which they interacted and were combined. It also happened that the S–R theorists were elementarists in the sense that they believed there were some fundamental 'simples' which were compounded in the complexities one ordinarily encountered, that they were mechanists in that they refused to accept teleological concepts as fundamental, that they were reductionist in that they believed that psychology was not merely related to biology but that in some way the former could in principle be derived from the latter, that they were peripheralists in that they stressed what happened on the surface of the organism – stimulation of its receptors and activity of its effectors – and that they were empiristic (or as it is often said environmentalist) in that they stressed the role of learning in establishing the S–R connexions of the mature higher organism. The cognitive theories asserted an epistemological distinction which the S–R theorists rejected either explicitly or implicitly, namely between the objective, independently existing world and the phenomenal world, the world as it seems to the organism. It was the latter that the cognitive theorists held to be the key to describing, explaining and predicting the behaviour of men and the other animals. It also happened that the cognitive theorists regarded this phenomenal world holistically. They regarded it as having a structure, as consisting of figures or bounded objects within a ground. They also regarded it as having field forces producing or tending to produce states of equilibrium. As a consequence, just as the S–R theorists concentrated on learning, the cognitive theorists concentrated on perception and creative thinking. Unlike the passive, elementarist content of the Wundtians, their phenomenalism was dynamic and holistic, and unlike the Wundtians they were less interested in phenomena in themselves, instead they saw them as the basis upon which behaviour was to be explained.

The dynamic depth theorists saw as the key motivational forces welling up from deep-lying sources. Though often regarded as having some physiological origins, motives were deemed to be strictly psychical – they were mental energies not physical energies, with their own distinctive way of working. They were seekings not pushings, that is, they were inherently directed to ends or goals and not merely channelled by mechanisms as physical

energy ordinarily is. Without espousing an extrinsic teleology, that is a view in which goals are deemed to be imposed from without, the dynamic depth theorists were
always in some sense teleological and anti-mechanistic.
Interestingly, at the one time they laid great stress on the
person, self or ego and insisted that a great deal goes on in
the mind of which the self has no cognizance. For Freud
this was the result of repression; for Janet and Morton
Prince it was the result of dissociation; for Jung it was in
part the inherited racial unconscious and so on. Among
the functionalists who were part of this movement, e.g.
McDougall and Rivers, roles for both repression and
dissociation were found and there was a tendency to avoid
painting a picture of as dark an unconscious mind as that
depicted by the psychoanalysts. Indeed terms like subconscious and co-conscious were preferred to unconscious. During the first half-century of the new empirical
psychology there was hardly a doubt that it was the
science of consciousness. Now from two sides that view
was challenged, the behaviourists saying that if there was
consciousness (other than discriminative responding) it
was not amenable to scientific study and the psychoanalysts saying that the conscious mind was only the relatively uncomplicated part of the iceberg above the
water and that the more significant part lay below the
surface, out of ordinary sight. Introspection, *the* method
of the early psychology, was thus held variously to be un-
reliable or to be only a verbal response or to be quite inadequate (trying to free a prisoner by applying a nail-file
and tooth-pick as it were). To those outside the dynamic
depth movement the emphasis on purposive psychic
forces and the unconscious, spoken of often as though it
were the hidden person with whom the self was in per-
petual contest, seemed to betoken mysticism and so to be
alien to science.

The differential theorists considered that the key to the
description, explanation and prediction of behaviour was
the typing of persons or alternatively their characterization

in terms of multivariate traits or dimensions. In the nineteen-twenties temperament was dealt with principally in typological terms, and consequently the movement was not incompatible with the dynamic depth view. Indeed many of the typologists were also members of that movement, for example Jung with his eightfold typology resulting from a distinction between the outward and inward turning of libido and from the predominance of one of the four functions, sensation, thinking, feeling and intuition in the person's mental operation, and Freud with his anal, oral and genital character types. Intelligence was, of course, being treated in multivariate or factorial terms primarily by Spearman and Burt in the United Kingdom but also by Truman Kelley who was later followed by Thurstone in America. The differential approach can be readily enough grafted on to any of the other approaches to human nature, but though it usually found a place in the early contemporary standard textbooks, it was being made largely independently of other approaches, a state of affairs that has continued to the present day.

In giving this thumb-nail sketch of the four types of psychology, their attitudes to some general issues have been mentioned. Among these are the molecular-molar alternative with the related issues concerning reductionism, emergentism and dualism. There is also the epistemological question, namely, are the objects of our knowledge mental, i.e., literally in and of the mind, or are they independently existing objects to which we respond? There is also the question of determinism. Contemporary psychology has generally been deterministic in the sense that it believes in and looks for causes of behaviour. S–R theory has tended to take an earlier mechanistic conception whereas cognitive theory has turned to field conceptions in modern physics. But neither physical model satisfies the dynamic depth theorist who insists on the reality and irreducibility of purposes or inherently directed organismic, if not purely psychic, forces.

There is another set of issues to do with what psychology as a branch of knowledge has as its task. The simplest is the positivist view that its task is descriptive, that laws are no more than generalizations of what has been observed and that prediction is essentially by way of extrapolation or based on the expectation that sequences and trends observed in the past will be repeated or will continue in comparable circumstances. The early S–R theorists tended to adopt this view and it has been the view of most of the multivariate differentialists and of some of the typologists. A more elaborate view is that there are laws of nature which though manifested in what may be observed are not merely the general trends in what may be observed. These laws are to be arrived at by hypothesis, by creative thinking and not merely by summarizing. They may be used in explanation and prediction in that they imply what has been observed and what will be observed. The Copernican theory of planetary motion as modified by Kepler may be cited as a descriptive theory whereas Newton's mechanics incorporating gravitation is an explanatory theory in the sense just specified. Some S–R theorists, and their number has increased in the contemporary period, most cognitive theorists and with some qualification the greater number of dynamic depth theorists have subscribed to the view that psychology should set out to be an explanatory science. There is a third view in which intuition, insight and understanding (in the sense of the German word *Verstehen*) are given a crucial role. There was a strong tendency to adopt it among the dynamic depth theorists, especially where they were affected by existentialism and a weaker tendency among those cognitive theorists in whom phenomenological thinking was dominant, and of course the continental typologists usually overtly avowed it.

This then is the way the psychological parties were divided and aligned at the beginning of the contemporary period.

Select Bibliography

General

E. G. Boring, *A History of Experimental Psychology*, Appleton-Century-Crofts, 2nd edition, 1950
The most comprehensive and scholarly history of modern psychology available in English; indispensable for any serious student of the subject.

E. G. Boring, *Sensation and Perception in the History of Experimental Psychology*, Appleton-Century, 1942
A valuable supplement to Boring's *History*.

E. G. Boring *et al.* (eds.), *A History of Psychology in Autobiography*, vol. 4, Clark U.P., 1952
(See C. Murchison, *A History of Psychology in Autobiography*, vols. 1, 2 and 3.)

W. Dennis (ed.), *Readings in the History of Psychology*, Appleton-Century-Crofts, 1948
Sixty-one selections ranging from Aristotle on memory and recollection, *circa* 330 B.C., to Hull on simple trial-and-error learning, 1930. Over half the selections are drawn from the period after 1850.

W. D. Ellis (ed.), *A Source Book of Gestalt Psychology*, Kegan Paul, Trench, Trubner & Co., 1938
An important collection of papers, most of them translated from German.

J. C. Flugel, *A Hundred Years of Psychology* (edition revised by D. J. West), Methuen, 1964
A brief account of the history of psychology since 1833, emphasising the period after 1860.

J. F. Fulton (ed.), *Selected Readings in the History of Physiology*, C. C. Thomas, 1930
Two of the eight sets of excerpts deal with the peripheral and central nervous systems and are relevant in the history of psychology.

L. S. Hearnshaw, *A Short History of British Psychology, 1840–1940*, Methuen, 1964

An important supplement to those histories of psychology which stress German and American thought.

E. Heidbreder, *Seven Psychologies*, Appleton-Century, 1933
An account of some of the main psychological movements deemed significant in the 1920s.

R. J. Herrnstein and E. G. Boring (eds.), *A Source Book in the History of Psychology*, Harvard U.P., 1965
One hundred and sixteen excerpts ranging from Aristotle on the five senses, *circa* 350 B.C., to Lashley on cerebral equipotentiality, 1929, organized under fifteen main headings.

G. Humphrey, *Thinking: an Introduction to its Experimental Psychology*, Methuen, 1951
Provides a valuable account of the thought experiments correcting the one-sided view provided by Titchener (1909).

C. Murchison (ed.), *Psychologies of 1925*, Clark U.P., 1928
C. Murchison (ed.), *Psychologies of 1930*, Clark U.P., 1930
A number of spokesmen for different psychologies presenting their cases.

C. Murchison (ed.), *A History of Psychology in Autobiography*, Clark U.P., vol. 1, 1930; vol. 2, 1932; vol. 3, 1936. (See Boring *et al.*, *A History of Psychology in Autobiography*, vol. 4)
A number of eminent psychologists record with varying degrees of illumination their life stories.

G. Murphy, *Historical Introduction to Modern Psychology*, Harcourt Brace, revised 1949
Provides a picture of substantially the same events as provided in Boring's *History* but drawn with broader strokes.

R. S. Peters (ed.), *Brett's History of Psychology*, George Allen & Unwin, 1953
The best single account in English of the long past of psychology.

B. Rand (ed.), *Classical Psychologists*, Houghton Mifflin, 1912
Forty-three sets of selections, translated into English where the original is in another language. Twelve are ancient and medieval, another twelve are pre-nineteenth-century and the remainder nineteenth-century.

R. I. Watson, *The Great Psychologists: from Aristotle to Freud*, Lippincott, 1963
An account of the views and the lives of a number of great men in the history of psychology. Six chapters are devoted

to ancient and medieval and three to early modern philosophers who helped shape modern psychology and eleven to those who formed modern psychology in the eighty years after 1850.

R. S. Woodworth, *Contemporary Schools of Psychology*, Holt, 1931, revised edition 1948
An account of some of the main psychological movements deemed significant in the 1920s.

G. Zilboorg and G. W. Henry, *A History of Medical Psychology*, Norton, 1941
Traces the history of thought about and treatment of mental disorder from the classical period through the medieval period to the rise of modern views in the seventeenth century and their culmination in the work on Freud and his contemporaries in the early twentieth century.

Main Works (to which reference, whether explicit or implicit, has been made in the text)

Alexander, S., *Space, Time and Deity*, London, Macmillan, 1920

Allport, G. W., *Personality, a psychological interpretation*, Holt, 1937

Angell, J. R., *Psychology: an introductory study of the structure and function of human consciousness*, Holt, 1904

Angell, J. R., 'The province of functional psychology', *Psychol. Rev.*, vol. 14 (1907)
Reprinted in W. Dennis (ed.), *Readings*

Bain, A., *The Senses and the Intellect*, Parker, 1855

Bain, A., *The Emotions and the Will*, Parker, 1859

Baird, J. W., 'The influence of accommodation and convergence upon the perception of depth', *Amer. J. Psychol.*, vol. 14 (1903)

Baldwin, J. M., *Mental Development in the Child and the Race*, New York, Macmillan, 1895

Baldwin, J. M., *Development and Evolution*, New York, Macmillan, 1902

Bell, C., *Idea of a New Anatomy of the Brain: submitted for the observation of his friends.* (Privately published, 1811)
Revised version reprinted in W. Dennis (ed.), *Readings*,

and in substantial part in J. F. Fulton (ed.), *Selected Readings*.

Berkeley, G., *An Essay towards a New Theory of Vision*, Dublin, Jeremy Pepyat, 1709

Binet, A., and Henri, V., 'La psychologie individuelle', *L'Année psychol.*, vol. 2 (1896)

Binet, A., and Simon, T., 'Sur la nécessité d'établir un diagnostic scientifique des états inférieurs de l'intelligence', *L'Année psychol.*, vol. 11 (1905)

Binet, A., and Simon, T., 'Sur la nécessité d'établir un diagnostic du niveau intellectuel des anormaux', *L'Année psyhol.*, vol. 11 (1905)

Binet, A., and Simon, T., 'Le développement de l'intelligence chez les enfants', *L'Année psychol.*, vol. 14 (1908)
    Trans. into English by E. S. Kite and reprinted in J. J. Jenkins and D. G. Paterson (eds.), *Studies in Individual Differences*, Appleton-Century-Crofts, 1961

Boring, E. G., *The Physical Dimensions of Consciousness*, Century, 1933

Braid, J., *Neurypnology*, Churchill, 1843

Brentano, F., *Psychologie vom empirischen Standpunkte*, Duncker and Humblot, 1874

Broca, P., 'Remarques sur la siège de la faculté du langage articulé, suivies d'une observation d'aphonie', *Bull. de la Société Anatomique de Paris* (1861)
    Excerpt trans. into English in R. J. Herrnstein and E. G. Boring (eds.), *A Source Book*

Burt, C., *Three Reports of the Distribution and Relations of Educational Abilities*, P. S. King, 1917

Burt, C., *The Factors of the Mind*, University of London Press, 1940

Calkins, M., *A First Book in Psychology*, New York, Macmillan, 1909

Cattell, J. McK., 'Mental tests and measurements', *Mind*, vol. 15 (1890)
    Reprinted in W. Dennis (ed.), *Readings*

Cattell, J. McK., 'The conceptions and methods of psychology', *Pop. Sci. Monthly*, vol. 66 (1904)

Charcot, J. M., *Oeuvres complètes*, Lecrosnier et Babé, 1890

Darwin, C., *The Origin of Species*, Murray, 1859

Darwin, C., *Expression of the Emotions in Man and Animal*, Murray, 1872

Descartes, R., *Discours de la méthode*, Leyde, 1637
Trans. into English by J. Veitch as *A Discourse on Method*, Dent, 1912

Descartes, R., *Les passions de l'âme*, Amsterdam, 1650
Trans. into English by E. S. Haldane and G. R. T. Ross in *The Philosophical Works of Descartes*, Cambridge U.P., 1931

Donders, F. C., 'Die Schnelligkeit psychischer Processe', *Arch. Anat. Physiol.* (1862)

Ebbinghaus, H., *Über das Gedächtnis*, Duncker and Humblot, 1885
Trans. into English by H. A. Ruger and C. Bussenius as *On Memory*, Columbia U.P., 1913

Ebbinghaus, H., *Abriss der Psychologie*, Veit; vol. 1, 1908; vol. 2, 1909; vol. 3, 1910

Von Ehrenfels, C., 'Über Gestaltqualitäten', *Vierteljahresshr. f. wiss. Phil.*, vol. 14 (1890)

Fechner, G., *Elemente der Psychophysik*, Breitkopf and Härtel, 1860
Vol. 1 trans. into English by H. E. Adler as *Elements of Psychophysics*, Holt, Rinehart and Winston, 1966

Flourens, P. J. M., *Recherches expérimentales sur les propriétés et les fonctions du système nerveux dans les animaux vertébrés*, Crevot, 1824
Excerpts trans. into English in J. F. Fulton (ed.), *Selected Readings*, in W. Dennis (ed.), *Readings*, and in R. J. Herrnstein and E. G. Boring (eds.), *A Source Book*

Freud, S., *Die Traumdeutung*, Deuticke, 1900
Rev. edns., 1909, 1911, 1914 and 1919
Trans. into English in *Complete Psychological Works of Sigmund Freud*, vol. 4, Hogarth, 1953

Freud, S., *Drei Abhandlungen zur Sexualtheorie*, Deuticke, 1905
Trans. into English, *Complete Psychological Works*, vol. 7

Freud, S., *Der Witz und seine Beziehung zum Unbewussten*, Deuticke, 1905
Trans. into English, *Complete Psychological Works*, vol. 8

Freud, S., *Totem und Tabu*, Heller, 1913
Trans. into English, *Complete Psychological Works*, vol. 13

Freud, S., 'Zur Geschichte der psychoanalytischen Bewegung', *Jahr. der Psychoanalyse*, vol. 6 (1914)
Trans. into English, *Complete Psychological Works*, vol. 14

Freud, S., *Vorlesungen zur Einführung in die Psychoanalyse*, Heller, 1917
Trans. into English, *Complete Psychological Works*, vols. 15 and 16

Freud, S., *Das Ich und das Es*, Internationaler Psychoanalytischer Verlag, 1923
Trans. into English, *Complete Psychological Works*, vol. 19

Fritsch, G. and Hitzig, E., 'Über die elektrische Erregbarkeit des Grosshirns', *Archiv. für Anatomie, Physiologie und wissenschaftliche Medizin* (1870), no. 48
Excerpt trans. into English in R. J. Herrnstein and E. G. Boring (eds.), *A Source Book*

Gall, F. J., *Sur les fonctions du cerveau et sur celles de chacune de ses parties*, vols. 4 and 6, Ballière, 1825
Trans. by W. Lewis as Gall's *Works*, vols. 4 and 6, Boston, 1835

Galton, F., *Hereditary Genius: an inquiry into its laws and consequences*, London, Macmillan, 1869

Galton, F., 'Co-relations and their Measurement, chiefly from Anthropometric Data', *Proc. Royal Soc.*, London, vol. 45 (1888), pp. 135–45
Reprinted in J. J. Jenkins and D. G. Paterson (eds.), *Studies in Individual Differences*

Galvani, A. L., *De viribus electricitatis in motu musculari commentarius*, Societas Typographica, 1791
Excerpt trans. into English in J. F. Fulton (ed.), *Selected Readings*

Goddard, H. H., *The Kallikak Family: a study in the heredity of feeblemindedness*, New York, Macmillan, 1912

Hall, G. S., *Adolescence*, Appleton, 1911

Hall, M., *New Memoir on the Nervous System*, Ballière, 1843

Hartley, D., *Observations on Man, his Frame, his Duty and his Expectations*, Bath, Leake and Frederick, 1749

Healy, W., and Fernald, G. M., 'Tests for practical mental classification', *Psychol. Monog.*, vol. 13 (1911)

von Helmholtz, H. (Note on rate of transmission of the nervous impulse), *Monatsberichte der Akademie der Wissenschaften zu Berlin*, 1850
Trans. into English in W. Dennis (ed.), *Readings*

von Helmholtz, H., *Handbuch der physiologischen Optik*, Leipzig; vol. 1, 1856; vol. 2, 1860; vol. 3, 1866

Trans. into English from 3rd edn., 1909, by J. P. C. Southall as *Helmholtz' Treatise on Physiological Optics*, Rochester, N.Y., 1924–25

von Helmholtz, H., *Die Lehre von den Tonempfindungen*, Vieweg & Sohn, 1863

Trans. into English by A. J. Ellis as *Sensations of Tone*, London, 1875

Hering, E., *Zur Lehre vom Lichtsinne*, Vienna, Akad. der Wissensch., 1878

Various excerpts trans. into English appear in R. J. Herrnstein and E. G. Boring (eds.), *A Source Book*, in B. Rand (ed.), *Classical Psychologists* and in R. C. Teevan and R. C. Birney (eds.), *Color Vision*, von Nostrand, 1961

Hillebrand, W., 'Das Verhältnis von Akkommodation und Konvergenz zur Tiefenlokalisation', *Z. Psychol.*, vol. 7 (1894)

Holt, E. B., *et al.*, *The New Realism*, New York, Macmillan, 1912

Hume, D., *A Treatise of Human Nature: being an attempt to introduce the experimental method of reasoning into moral subjects*, Bk 1, London, Noon, 1739

Hunter, W. S., *General Psychology*, University of Chicago Press, 1919

Husserl, E., *Logische Untersuchungen*, Niemeyer, 1900

Jackson, J. Hughlings, *The Evolution and Dissolution of the Nervous System*, Croonian Lectures, London, 1884

James, W., *Principles of Psychology*, 2 vols., London, Macmillan, 1890

James, W., 'Does consciousness exist?', *J. Philos., Psychol. and sci. Method*, vol. 1 (1904), no. 18

Reprinted in W. James, *Essays in Radical Empiricism*, New York, Longmans, Green, 1912

Janet, P., *Les Obsessions et la Psychasténie*, Alcan, 1903

Janet, P., *La Force et la Faiblesse psychologique*, Maloine, 1932

Katz, D., 'Die Erscheinungsweisen der Farben und ihre Beeinflussung durch die individuelle Erfahrung', *Z. Psychol.*, Ergbd 7 (1911)

Kelley, T. L., *Crossroads in the Mind of Man: a study of differential mental abilities*, Stanford U.P., 1928

Chap. 1 reprinted in J. J. Jenkins and D. G. Paterson (eds.), *Studies in Individual Differences*

Koffka, K., *Principles of Gestalt Psychology*, Kegan Paul, Trench, Trubner, 1935

Köhler, W., *Intelligenzprüfungen an Anthropoiden*, Berlin, Akad. d. Wissensch., 1917

Trans. from 2nd rev. edn into English by E. Winter as *The Mentality of Apes*, Kegan Paul, 1925

Köhler, W., *Gestalt Psychology*, New York, Liveright, 1929

Kraepelin, E., *Psychiatrie: Ein Lehrbuch für Studierende und Aerzte*, Leipzig, Barth, 1899

Trans. into English from 6th edn by A. Ross Defendorf as *Clinical Psychiatry*, New York and London, Macmillan, 1902

Külpe, O., *Grundriss der Psychologie*, Leipzig, Engelmann, 1893

Trans. into English by E. B. Titchener as *Outlines of Psychology*, New York, Macmillan, 1895

Ladd, G. T., *Elements of Physiological Psychology*, Scribner, 1887

Rev. edn with R. S. Woodworth, 1911

Ladd, G. T., *Primer of Psychology*, Scribner, 1894

Lewin, K., *A Dynamic Theory of Personality: Selected papers*, McGraw-Hill, 1935

Locke, J., *An Essay concerning Human Understanding:* in four books, London, Thos. Basset, 1690

McDougall, W., *An Introduction to Social Psychology*, Methuen, 1908

McDougall, W., *An Outline of Psychology*, Methuen, 1923

McDougall, W., *An Outline of Abnormal Psychology*, Methuen, 1926

Magendie, F., 'Expériences sur les fonctions des racines des nerfs rachidiens', *Jour. Physiol. expér. et path.*, vol. 2 (1822)

Magendie, F., 'Expériences sur les fonctions des racines des nerfs qui naissent de la moelle épinière', ibid.

Trans. in J. F. Fulton (ed.), *Selected Readings*

Mill, James, *Analysis of the Phenomena of the Human Mind*, Baldwin and Craddock, 1829

New edn with notes by A. Bain, A. Findlater and G. Grote, edited with additional notes by J. S. Mill, Longmans, Green, Reader and Dyer, 1869. Reprinted 1878

Morgan, C. Lloyd, *Introduction to Comparative Psychology*, London, Scott, 1894

Morgan, C. Lloyd, *Animal Behaviour*, Arnold, 1900

Müller, G. E., *Zur Grundlegung der Psychophysik*, Hofmann, 1879

Müller, G. E., 'Zur Psychophysik der Gesichtsempfindungen', *Z. Psychol.*, vol. 10 (1896)
Reproduced in part in trans. in R. J. Herrnstein and E. G. Boring (eds.), *A Source Book*

Müller, J., *Handbuch der Physiologie des Menschen*, published in parts, 1834–40, Hölscher
Trans. into English by W. Baly as *Elements of Physiology*, London, Taylor & Walton; vol. 1, 1838; vol. 2, 1842

Pavlov, I. P., *Conditioned reflexes*, Oxford U.P., 1927
Trans. by G. V. Anrep from the Russian original

Perry, R. B., *The Thought and Character of William James*, Little, Brown, 1935

Rahn, C., 'The relation of sensation to other categories in contemporary psychology', *Psychol. Monog.*, vol. 16 (1913)

Reid, T., *Essays on the Intellectual Powers of Man*, Edinburgh, 1785

Romanes, G. J., *Animal Intelligence*, Kegan Paul, 1881

Romanes, G. J., *Mental Evolution in Animals*, Kegan Paul, 1883

Romanes, G. T., *Mental Evolution in Man: origin of human faculty*, Kegan Paul, 1888

Rubin, E., *Synsoplevede Figurer: Studier i psykologisk Analyse*, Copenhagen, Gyldendahl, 1915

Schumann, F., 'Beiträge zur Analyse der Gesichtswarnehmungen' (4 parts), *Z. Psychol.*, vols. 23, 24, 30 and 36, 1900–1904

Spearman, C., 'The proof and measurement of association between two things', *Amer. J. Psychol.*, vol. 15 (1904)
Reprinted in J. J. Jenkins and D. G. Paterson (eds.), *Studies in Individual Differences*

Spearman, C., ' "General Intelligence" objectively determined and measured', *Amer. J. Psychol.*, vol. 15 (1904)
Reprinted in J. J. Jenkins and D. G. Paterson (eds.), *Studies in Individual Differences*

Spearman, C., *The Abilities of Man: their nature and assessment*, London, Macmillan, 1927

Stern, W., *Allgemeine Psychologie auf personalistischer Grundlage*, The Hague, Nijhoff, 1935
Trans. into English by H. D. Spoerl as *General Psychology from the personalistic standpoint*, New York, Macmillan, 1938

Stout, G. F., *Analytic Psychology*, Sonnenschein, 1896

Stout, G. F., *A Manual of Psychology*, Clive; vol. 1, 1898; vol. 2, 1899; 3rd edn, 1913; 4th edn, 1929

Stout, G. F., *A Groundwork of Psychology*, Clive, 1903

Stumpf, C., *Tonpsychologie*, Hirzel; vol. 1, 1883; vol. 2, 1890
An excerpt trans. into English appears in B. Rand (ed.), *Classical Psychologists*

Theophrastos, [*Characters*] *circa* early 3rd century B.C.
The thirty 'characters' which have been preserved trans. into English by R. Aldington in *A Book of Characters*, Routledge, 1924

Thomson, G. H., 'A hierarchy without a general factor', *Brit. J. Psychol.*, vol. 8 (1916)

Thorndike, E. L., 'Animal intelligence', *Psychol. Rev. Monog. Supp.*, 2 (1898)

Thorndike, E. L., *Educational Psychology*, Columbia U.P., 1913

Titchener, E. B., *Primer of Psychology*, New York, Macmillan, 1898

Titchener, E. B., *Experimental Psychology: a manual of laboratory practice*, New York, Macmillan; vol. 1, Qualitative experiments pts 1 and 2, 1901; vol. 2, Quantitative experiments pts 1 and 2, 1905

Titchener, E. B., *Lectures on the Experimental Psychology of the Thought-Processes*, New York, Macmillan, 1909

Titchener, E. B., *A Textbook of Psychology*, New York, Macmillan, 1909

Titchener, E. B., *Systematic Psychology: Prolegomena*, New York, Macmillan, 1929

Ward, J., 'Psychology', *Encyclopaedia Brittanica*, 9th edn, 1866

Watson, J. B., 'Psychology as the behaviorist views it', *Psychol. Rev.*, vol. 20 (1913)
Reprinted in W. Dennis (ed.), *Readings*

Watson, J. B., *Behavior: an introduction to comparative psychology*, Holt, 1914

Watson, J. B., *Psychology from the Standpoint of a Behaviorist*, Lippincott, 1919

Weber, E. H., *De pulsu, resorptione, auditu et tactu: annotationes anatomical et physiological*, Leipzig, 1834
The passages dealing with the Weber fraction appear in trans. in R. J. Herrnstein and E. G. Boring (eds.), *A Source Book*

Wertheimer, M., 'Experimentelle Studien über das Sehen von Bewegung', *Z. Psychol.* (1912), no. 61
Trans. in part into English in T. Shipley (ed.), *Classics in Psychology*, New York, 1961

Wertheimer, M., 'Untersuchungen zur Lehre von der Gestalt', *Psychol. Forsch.*, vol. 4 (1923)
Trans. into English in part in W. D. Ellis (ed.), *A Source Book of Gestalt Psychology*, Kegan Paul, Trench, Trubner, 1938

Whytt, R., *An Essay on the Vital and other Involuntary Motions of Animals*, Hamilton, Balfour and Neill, 1751
Excerpt in J. F. Fulton (ed.), *Selected Readings* and in R. S. Herrnstein and E. G. Boring (eds.), *A Source Book*

Wissler, C., 'Correlation of mental and physical tests', *Psychol. Monog.*, vol. 16 (1901)
Reprinted in J. J. Jenkins and D. G. Paterson (eds.), *Studies in Individual Differences*

Woodworth, R. S., *Dynamic Psychology*, Columbia U.P., 1918

Woodworth, R. S., *Psychology, a study of mental life*, 1st edn, Holt, 1921

Wundt, W. M., *Beiträge zur Theorie der Sinneswahrnehmung*, Leipzig, Winter, 1858–62

Wundt, W. M., *Vorlesungen über die Menschen – und Tierseele*, Leipzig, Voss, 1st edn, 1863; Hamburg, Voss, 2nd rev. edn, 1892
2nd edn trans. into English by J. E. Creighton and E. B. Titchener as *Lectures on Human and Animal Psychology*, Sonnenschein, 1894

Wundt, W. M., *Grundzüge der physiologischen Psychologie*, Kroner; 1st edn, 1874; 7th edn, 1923
Portion of 5th edn trans. into English by E. B. Titchener as *Principles of Physiological Psychology*, New York, Macmillan, 1904

Wundt, W. M., *Grundriss der Psychologie*, Engelmann, 1896
Trans. into English by C. H. Judd as *Outlines of Psychology*, Stechert, 1897

Wundt, W. M., *Völkerpsychologie: eine Untersuchung der Entwicklungsgesetze von Sprache, Mythus und Sitte*, Engelmann; vol. 1, 1900 (expanded into vol. 1, 1911 and vol. 2, 1912); vol. 2, 1905–6 (expanded into vol. 3, 1908 and vol. 4, 1910); vol. 5, 1914; vol. 6, 1915; vol. 7, 1917; vol. 8, 1917; vol. 9, 1918; vol. 10, 1920

Wundt, W. M., *Elemente der Völkerpsychologie*, Kroner, 1912
  Trans. into English by E. L. Schaub as *Elements of Folk Psychology*, Allen and Unwin, 1916
Young, T., 'On the theory of light and colours', *Philos. Trans. Royal Soc.*, London, 1802
  Reprinted in W. Dennis (ed.), *Readings*

Index

Penguin Science of Behaviour

Other titles available in this series include:

Assessment in Clinical Psychology
C. E. Gathercole

This book offers an introduction and a framework to some of
the main issues of assessment, and describes some of the
problems with which psychiatrists and others present the
clinical psychologist.
X14/6s

Disorders of Memory and Learning
George A. Talland

This important work analyses disorders of memory and
learning in relation to normal learning and memory.
X35/6s

Psychometric Assessment
of the Individual Child
R. Douglas Savage

This book covers the assessment of intellectual, educational,
personality and motor-perceptual characteristics, and is
completed by examples of the comprehensive assessment
undertaken on some typical clinical-educational problem
children.
X15/6s

Penguin Modern Psychology

This series of Readings complements the *Penguin Science of Behaviour* series in providing for the student collections of papers that can be used as primary sources or as background material. The Readings are selected and introduced by leading psychologists.

Titles already available are: